Schneider, Eberhard, 1941-
    The G.D.R : the history, politics, economy, and
society of East Germany / by Eberhard Schneider ;
translated ₍from the German₎ by Hannes Adomeit and
Roger Clarke. --   London : C. Hurst, 1978.
    xii ₍i.e. 13₎, 121 p. ; 23 cm.

    Translation of Die DDR.
    Includes index.
    Bibliography: p. 118.
    LC: 79307635   ISBN: 0905838025 : £6.50

    1. Germany, East. I. Title.

895

THE G.D.R.

THE G.D.R.

The History, Politics, Economy and Society
of East Germany

BY

EBERHARD SCHNEIDER

TRANSLATED BY

HANNES ADOMEIT and ROGER CLARKE

C. HURST & COMPANY · LONDON

First published in English by
C. Hurst & Co. (Publishers) Ltd.,
1-2 Henrietta Street, London WC2E 8PS, England

German edition *Die DDR : Geschichte, Politik, Wirtschaft,
Gesellschaft* (1st edition) © 1975, Verlag Bonn Aktuell GmbH, Stuttgart
This edition © 1978, C. Hurst & Co. (Publishers) Ltd.
ISBN 0-905838-02-5

Typeset by Red Lion Setters,
Holborn, London and
printed in Great Britain by
Billing and Sons Ltd., Guildford,
London and Worcester

Contents

ERRATA

Introduction

The German Democratic Republic came into being as a successor-state to the former Soviet zone of occupation, closely following the Soviet model of organisation in state and society.This came about once the Western powers had demonstrated their determination to create in the western parts of Germany a state which could safeguard the rule of law and secure basic human rights, at least for the majority of the German population. The first step taken in this direction was the 1948 currency reform in West Germany. This was a sign that the West was no longer willing to stop on the path along which it had begun to progress.

The aims of Soviet policy in Germany and Europe were diametrically opposed to those of the Western powers. Originally, the division of Germany had not been one of Stalin's preferences because it appeared to him to be more important to have access to the economy of the whole of Germany (including, principally, the Ruhr) for the purpose of reconstruction in the USSR with the aid of German reparation payments. In that phase of Soviet policy, Stalin would probably have been prepared to draw a distinction between Germany, on the one hand, and those European countries already firmly integrated into the Soviet bloc on the other. If this had come about, this policy could have combined short-term or medium-term co-operation with the Western allies for the purpose of controlling Germany as a military or political factor in the centre of Europe, while benefiting from German economic potential.

The Western powers did not appreciate the different treatment afforded to Germany as opposed to that to which the East European countries were subjected. Instead, against the background of the Berlin blockade, the Communist coup in Czechoslovakia and Soviet opposition to Western policy in Germany, the Western powers came to the conclusion that Stalin wanted to establish a Communist regime in the Soviet Occupation Zone in Germany (just as he had done in the East European countries) and that he intended to use this regime gradually to extend the Soviet sphere of influence to cover all of Europe.

Whereas the Western powers had begun to lay the foundations for the separate development of West Germany when they decreed the currency reform in 1948, it would be true to say that separate development in the Soviet Occupation Zone had begun three years earlier with the establishment of a political structure which found

vii

no parallel in the three Western zones. To that extent, the Western allies were only following the Soviet example when they authorized the Prime Ministers of the eleven German *Länder* to draft a Constitution which would be valid 'temporarily' in the three Western zones. The foundation of the two German states in 1949 merely institutionalized the two separate paths of development taken by the two parts of Germany after the war.

In nearly three decades since it came into existence, the GDR has advanced, despite difficult starting conditions, to a medium-ranking power of economic and political importance and, within the Eastern economic community Comecon, to the second most important economic factor with the highest standard of living in Eastern Europe. The not inconsiderable achievements of the population of the GDR become apparent only by comparison with the other Eastern European countries under 'real socialism', not necessarily *vis-à-vis* the Federal Republic.

The opportunity to compare the political systems of East and West presents itself temptingly in the two Germanies, since nowhere else in Europe have the two politically and economically antagonistic orders been established on the territory of a previously uniform state and with people of the same nation. The citizens of these two different systems have the same historical and cultural background and the same techno-professional training standards with the same abilities and skills. Here the structure and effect of the two different systems can be studied most distinctly, without having to make allowance for differences of mentality or nationality as would be necessary, for example, if one attempted to compare the systems of Poland and France or Czechoslovakia and Great Britain. A comparison, furthermore, is only feasible on a basis such as that common to both German states. The *Bericht der Bundesregierung und Materialen zur Lage der Nation 1971* (Federal Government Report and Material on the State of the Nation 1971) establishes three common factors shared by the two German states: 'Both of the German economic and social systems are efficiency-orientated, . . . geared towards growth and modernization, . . . [and] are characterized by the increasing importance of science, research, education and training.'

The author does not attempt here to undertake a comparison of the two systems. He has chosen a composite method for his presentation, combining the analysis and interpretation of the GDR as seen from within the system with a critical appraisal from a vantage point outside it. The point of reference of the description from within the system is the GDR's conception of its own identity. To counter the danger of adopting this conception uncritically, the author has introduced an appraisal from the point of view of a different system, based on the values held in Western-type parliamentary democracies.

The author does not restrict himself to describing facts and functions to point out similarities to and differences from the West German system. The inherent danger in undertaking a study in this way is that of attempting to compare features for which there is no comparison; for the political system of the GDR is, in its entirety and in its various sub-systems, comprehensible in the last analysis only on the basis of its ideological values and goals.

Furthermore, as a general principle, more political importance is attributed to the ideological factor in the GDR than in the other states of Eastern Europe. Quite apart from the fact that the ideology is the only legitimation for the existence of the East European governing Communist Parties and for their claim to leadership, the GDR is obliged to resort to an even greater extent to its ideology in order to differentiate itself from the Federal Republic of Germany and to substantiate its separate identity. Unlike the other states of Eastern Europe, the GDR is not in a position to appeal to national values, for all such factors — language, history, culture, manners and customs — it shares with the Federal Republic. Only in its ideological pretensions and in the specific political character of its system is it fundamentally different from the Federal Republic.

In foreign policy, the GDR is not considered to be a responsible factor comparable to the Federal Republic of Germany, for it lacks the economic and technological potential of the West German state. It derives its foreign-policy significance from the unanimity of the 'socialist camp' under the leadership of the Soviet Union. For the GDR, the identity of interests between the USSR and the GDR is accounted for from the security policy point of view by the desire of the two states not to allow the re-unification of Germany. From the Soviet point of view, the identity of the Soviet interests with those of the GDR is born of considerations of military strategy and bloc politics.

As a loyal ally, the GDR, which plays host to a contingent of Soviet troops twice as strong as its own national army, follows the Soviet anti-Chinese and pro-Palestinian (pro-PLO) line. Though charged by the Communist Party of the Soviet Union with making arrangements for the European Conference of the Communist Parties in East Berlin in 1976, the preparations for which proved very difficult, the Socialist Unity Party of Germany (SED), and thus the GDR, by virtue of its complete lack of detailed political comments of its own, has still to this day not joined in the condemnation of Eurocommunism.

The identity of its interests with those of the Soviet Union, which is vital to the GDR's very existence, harbours a certain aspect of competition between the two since the Soviet Union is concerned with displacing the GDR from its status as a privileged partner

when implementing Bonn's *Ostpolitik* in concrete terms. And
conversely: since the conclusion of the Moscow agreement between
the Soviet Union and the Federal Republic of Germany, the GDR
has been engaged in futile competition with the Federal Republic to
gain the USSR's favour as a privileged partner for the supply of
modern technological know-how.

Even conflicts on a limited scale are inevitable between the GDR
and the USSR if the GDR offers resistance to Soviet intentions on
the grounds that these would jeopardize its internal security. The
USSR is forced to accept such arguments, unless this affects central
Soviet interests. For since the Czechoslovakia crisis of 1968, the
USSR has become much more cautious in its dealings with the
countries of Eastern Europe. Since then it has been affording them
a bigger say in affairs and has been making an effort to pay more
attention to their individual interests. Seen against the background
of Stalin's offer, made in the 1950s, of consent to the re-unification
of Germany, it must not be overlooked, when assessing relations
between the GDR and the USSR in general, that for the GDR the
question of the future of Germany is a question of to be or not to
be, but for the USSR it is regional matter, though admittedly an
extremely complex one and one of great political consequence.

Until the GDR achieved worldwide recognition in 1972, its
foreign policy was geared towards undermining the Federal Republic's claim to the sole right to represent Germany as a whole. With
this intention in mind, the GDR approached the Arab states and
some black African and South Asian countries seeking diplomatic
recognition and admission to the United Nations. In this it achieved
only moderate success, but since achieving this goal, the GDR has,
within the framework of the common foreign policy of the
members of the Warsaw Pact, been evolving various foreign policy
activities *vis-à-vis* a number of Scandinavian and Western
European countries and Japan.

Until now, its membership of the United Nations has not given
the GDR cause to play a part in the solution of the North-South
problem by making its own conceptual proposals. Rather one
gathers the impression that some division of foreign policy labour
among the Warsaw Pact states has given the GDR tasks in Third
World countries, which it appears to be eminently capable of
performing. The GDR's development aid policy is centred on the
Arab states, a number of black African countries and India. At the
comparatively low level of development aid which it provides,
ensuring a supply of raw materials for itself at a low price is high
among the GDR's considerations.

The self-avowed supreme objective of the GDR's foreign policy
is 'to secure favourable conditions for the construction of socialism
at home'. This ideologically motivated domestic policy imposes

restrictions on foreign policy, under which is included policy towards the other German state, for the GDR can only implement its pan-German and détente policies to the extent that its socio-political *status quo* can cope with the many-faceted aperture expected in this context as a *quid pro quo*. The favourable conditions for the 'construction of socialism' which are to be secured by foreign policy activity are not meant to apply only to the GDR itself: there is a perceptible revolutionary class struggle dimension to the GDR's foreign policy. The fundamental ideo-logical antithesis to capitalism inherent in the foreign policy of the second German state leads the GDR into antagonism towards the countries of the West, and in particular towards the Federal Republic. The objective — born of necessity out of this basic ideological position — of diminishing the international political influence of the West German state, and thus its influence on the population of the GDR is counterbalanced by the attractive economic conditions offered by the West Germans, conditions which the GDR could only afford to turn down at great sacrifice.

Although the GDR leadership has solemnly forsworn the desire for re-unification, this desire is still alive mong the population of the GDR, even more actively so than among the West Germans. The citizens of the GDR link this desire with their hopes of a change in the political system at present in force, which they feel to be oppressive. No matter how such a convergence of the two German states might come about, if it were able to do so at all, the population of the second German state is convinced that the result of this process — which at present, if on a dispassionate assessment, appears politically somewhat unrealistic — is still bound to be better, simply because it is likely to be more liberal than the present strictly authoritarian order.

The internal situation in the GDR and its relations with the Federal Republic are not simply an internal German affair but are of great importance to East-West relations as a whole. This is because the two military, economic, political and ideological constellations and systems meet eye-to-eye at the German-German border. All shifts in relations between the two German states have their repercussions on the relationship between East and West, and vice versa; all transitions in East-West relations expand or contract the margin within which relations between the Federal Republic of Germany and the German Democratic Republic can be improved.

The author would like to express his thanks to Hannes Adomeit and Roger Clarke for their translation. For the financial support provided by the Bundesinstitut für ostwissenschaftliche und inter-nationale Studien, Cologne, for the translation, the author is obliged to the Scientific Directorate and to the Director of the Institute. The Federal Ministry for Intra-German Relations kindly provided up-to-date statistical material.

1
Economic Geography

Territory

The German Democratic Republic, with a territory of 108,178 square km., lies in the centre of Europe. To the north its border is the Baltic Sea, to the east Poland, to the south Czechoslovakia and to the west the Federal German Republic. The total length of its land frontiers is 2,431.3 km., of which 1,381 km. form the border with the Federal Republic. In addition, it has a border of 160.5 km. with West Berlin.

Following the break-up of the province of Prussia by decision of the Allied Control Commission after the Second World War, the following five provinces were formed:

— Mecklenburg: consisting of Mecklenburg, parts of the former county of Stettin and the parts of the district of Dannenberg in the county of Lüneberg lying east of the Elbe.
— Brandenburg: consisting of the county of Potsdam and parts of the former county of Frankfurt on the Oder.
— Saxony-Anhalt: consisting of the parts of Saxony situated west of the Neisse and the former county of Liegnitz.
— Thuringen: consisting of Thuringia with the county of Erfurt and the district of Schmalkalden in the county of Kassel.
— The area of Greater Berlin retained the boundaries which had been established in 1920. Its twenty urban districts were divided into four sectors.[1]

On the basis of the 'Law on the further democratisation of the structure and mode of operation of state organs in the provinces of the GDR' of 23 July 1952, the provinces were abolished and replaced by counties, as shown on page 2 (figures for 31 December 1976).

Under this central administrative reform Greater Berlin, which was previously one administrative unit, received the status of a county. Parts of economic regions which had previously been politically and administratively separate were brought together, so that, for example, the parts of the Niederlausitz brown coalfield round Senftenberg and Hoyerswerde, previously subordinated to the provinces of Brandenburg, Sachsen and Sachsen-Anhalt, were incorporated into the county of Cottbus. Rural districts were increased in number from 120 to 191 and urban districts from 20 to 28. Each rural distict now contained some 50 parishes, compared with up to 100 and more previously.

1

County	Area (square km.)	Inhabitants
Berlin (East)	403	1,106,267
Cottbus	8,262	874,007
Dresden	6,738	1,825,816
Erfurt	7,349	1,238,231
Frankfurt/Oder	7,186	690,230
Gera	4,004	737,228
Halle	8,771	1,863,500
Karl-Marx-Stadt	6,009	1,962,233
Leipzig	4,966	1,435,424
Magdeburg	11,525	1,283,359
Neubrandenburg	10,792	625,058
Potsdam	12,572	1,117,104
Rostock	7,074	871,226
Schwerin	8,672	589,103
Suhl	3,856	548,244
GDR total	108,179	16,767,030[2]

Natural population trends

The population of the GDR on 31 December 1976 was 16,767,030.
The GDR territory, then the Soviet Occupation Zone, reached its
highest population figure in 1947, at 18.1 million. That this figure
exceeded that of the 1939 (16.7 million) despite the heavy losses of
the war is explained by the large number of refugees from the
former eastern regions of Germany who were settled in central
Germany. The population then declined till 1961, since when it has
risen again slightly. Today, with a territory nearly half that of the
Federal Republic (43.5%), the GDR has a population equal to
about 27% of that of the Federal Republic.

Up until the building of the wall on 13 August 1961, 2.7 million
people left the GDR, of whom 60% (from 1949 to 1961) were
members of the working population, and of whom some 620,000
were previously occupied in industry and skilled crafts (about 23%
of all refugees).

Because of the losses and the shortfall in births caused by the
war, the age structure pyramids in both parts of Germany are
similar, although there are certain differences which should not be
overlooked. The proportion of persons of working age (men from
15 to 65, women from 15 to 60) is smaller in the GDR than in the
Federal Republic (GDR: 1976 — 60.6%, FRG: 1974 — 60.9%) and
the proportion of pensioners (people above those ages) is higher
(GDR: 1976 — 19.3%, FRG: 1974 — 17.6%).

As well as the aging of the population of the GDR, the imbalance
between the sexes is also striking. Women outnumber men in the
proportion of 115 to 100. In 1976 the birth rate (live births per

1,000 inhabitants) was 11.6 in the GDR and 9.8 in the FRG. The place of the GDR was fourth from last in Europe. This low birth rate corresponds to the decline in marriages and is also attributable to the small numbers in the age groups born between 1942 and 1946. As a result of measures of encouragement devised by the state an increase in the birth rate since 1976 is in evidence.

After a marked peak in 1950 the number of marriages declined until 1968 and since then has been rising slightly. In 1976 there were 8.6 marriages and 2.7 divorces per 1000 inhabitants in the GDR, and in the FRG 5.9 and 1.5 respectively. Consequently the proportion of divorcees in the population of the same age is higher for all age groups in the GDR than in the Federal Republic.

Because of the unfavourable age structure the death rate in the GDR at 14.0 (1976) is also higher than in the FRG (11.9). This trend was not even halted by the rapid fall in infant mortality, which in 1976 was 1.4 per 100 live births in the GDR and 2.3 (1974) in the Federal Republic. The average life expectancy of the newly-born has risen at the same time and in 1974 was 74 for women and 69 for men in the GDR and in 1970-2 was 74 for women and 67 for men in the Federal Republic.

Population density and settlement pattern

The population density in the GDR is considerably lower than in the FRG: in 1976 it was 156 inhabitants per square kilometre in the GDR and 247 in the FRG. It is thus about one-third lower in the GDR than in the Federal Republic. The sparse settlement of the northern regions of the GDR is the result of its former agrarian structure, with large estates. In comparison with 1969, three counterbalancing regional changes in the growth of population in the GDR can be observed:

— above-average population growth in the three northern counties of Rostock, Schwerin and Neubrandenburg;
— slight population decline in the counties of Berlin, Magdeburg, Dresden, Leipzig and Karl-Marx-Stadt;
— little change in the population figures of the remaining counties.

Although a clear urbanisation process can be observed, no marked fragmentation of settlement in the GDR has been noticeable. In 1976, 6.0% of the population lived in communities of under 500 inhabitants (FRG — 1.4%), which accounted for 43.0% of all settlements (FRG — 28.6%). In 1976 25.0% of the GDR's population lived in communities of more than 100,000 inhabitants (FRG — 34.8%).

The three largest cities in the GDR had the following populations on 31 December 1976: East Berlin — 1,106,267; Leipzig — 564,596; Dresden — 510,408.

Occupation structure

The participation rate has risen continuously in the GDR, in contrast to the Federal Republic, and is today one of the highest in the world (GDR [1976] — 47.8%, FRG — 41.8%). At 82.6%, the proportion of women between the ages of 15 and 60 in employment is substantially higher than in the Federal Republic, where it is only 53.8%. Attempts have been made to overcome the labour shortage in the GDR by limited recruitment of about 50,000 'guest-workers' from Poland and Hungary. When the age structure of men of working age is examined, the considerably lower proportion of the middle age groups (25 to 50 years) in the GDR (46.7%) than in the FRG (51.3%) is striking. On the other hand, working pensioners are more significant in the GDR than in the Federal Republic. Cyclical unemployment is ruled out by the system which prevails in the GDR. The preservation of jobs, or overstaffing, is considered more important than rationalisation (the result is high production costs). Here it should be added that the percentage of self-employed in the working population of the GDR is far smaller than in the Federal Republic.

The occupation structure in the GDR is on the whole similar to that in the Federal Republic. In industry, mining, electricity generation and productive handicrafts the same percentage of people are employed in both German states. In the GDR 10.95% of the labour force was employed in agriculture in 1976, but only 6.3% in the Federal Republic (in 1976). The higher proportion of employment in agriculture is explained by the large number of immigrants after the Second World War and by the introduction of agricultural producers' cooperatives. Rather more people are employed in trade and services in the Federal Republic than in the GDR. On the other hand, because of the high level of private car ownership in the Federal Republic, fewer people are engaged in transport than in the GDR.[3] The same is true in the field of information distribution.

Because of the emigration of graduates from the GDR, the supply of highly-qualified labour there in the 1960s was inferior to that in the other German state. Since then the proportion is likely to have equalised, if it has not in fact swung in favour of the GDR. Comparison between higher education graduates in the two German states by specialisation and profession shows that in the GDR the natural sciences and technical specialisations have a higher place than in the Federal Republic.

The GDR achieved a forty-five-hour week for all workers in

1966, and in 1967 a five-day week was introduced, again for all workers. At first, workers in the GDR had to make up the time lost on Saturdays by overtime, which has since been abolished. Today all workers in the GDR have to work 43¾ hours per week.

Industry

The GDR stands in fifth place among industrial countries. In 1976, 59.1% of its national income production was generated by industry. The planned continuous concentration of industrial enterprises caused their number to diminish from around 18,300 in 1956 to around 13,160 enterprises of various sizes in 1967. At the same time the number of large enterprises with over 1,000 employees was growing and reached 578 in 1967.

The position regarding the generation of electricity by primary energy sources in 1976 was as follows: in first place as an energy source is unprocessed lignite, providing 82.0%; then follow mineral oil: 3.3%; hydro: 1.3%; hard coal: 0.6%; brown coal brickettes: 0.9%; other fuels: 11.9%. The counties of Cottbus, Dresden, Leipzig and Frankfurt on the Oder are electricity surplus regions. The county of Cottbus, where there is a modern plant for brown coal enrichment, can be seen as the centre of electricity generation in the GDR. As well as the Lausitz district in Cottbus brown coal is also surface-mined in central Germany in the district between Dessau, Halle, Merseburg, Altenburg, Borna, Leipzig and Torgau. In order to save transport costs power stations with capacities of up to 3,000 megawatts are under construction in the immediate neighbourhood of these open-cast brown coal mines.

The GDR has only a few minor hard coal areas, with small reserves. Since mining conditions are unfavourable, production costs are high. Furthermore, the quality of hard coal is mostly not suited to the production of metallurgical coke, so that mining is gradually being run down. Natural gas has been sought eagerly in the GDR, but so far gas production is small. Likewise, crude oil extraction is insignificant and the GDR has to import 90% of its total crude oil requirements from the USSR, and recently it has also imported oil from the Arab countries. The GDR is supplied with natural gas via a large Soviet pipeline, to which a grid system is connected for the northern counties which produce very little electric power themselves. The share of nuclear power in energy production was to rise from 0.2% in 1970 to 1.5% in 1975 and 4% in 1980.

The GDR is poor in iron ore deposits. The fact that the reserves are distributed among many deposits, unfavourable conditions of extraction, the iron content of only 20-35% of the ore and the thinness of the deposits make mining difficult and not very profitable. Iron ore mining in the GDR today is concentrated primarily in the Thuringian forest, the Harz, the Harz foothills and the Erzgebirge. The metals needed for the production of high-quality steel are also rare in the GDR. Of the nickel, manganese, wolfram, molybdenum and vanadium deposits to be found in the country, only certain nickel, manganese and wolfram deposits are of economic significance. Of the GDR's pig iron 60% is produced at the Eisenhüttenkombinat Ost in Eisenhüttenstadt on the Oder, 25% in the Max-Hütte in Unterwellenborn near Saalfeld and 15% in the Niederschachtofenwerk Calbe. Eisenhüttenstadt on the Oder was constructed in the neighbourhood of the former county town of Fürstenberg: the proximity of the Oder-Spree canal made it possible to build an ore and coal port. The majority of the iron ore needed is supplied by the Soviet Union, and the hard coal also comes from the USSR, as well as from Poland and Czechoslovakia. Steel is produced in the GDR in Brandenburg, Henningsdorf, Gröditz, Riesa, Freital, Thale and Unterwellenborn.

In the non-ferrous metals industry the GDR can rely on domestic ores; although she has to turn to imports for aluminium, there are deposits of copper, lead, zinc and tin ores within the country. Copper is mined on the edges of the Harz and the Thuringian forest, lead and zinc in the south-east of the Harz and Freiburg areas, and tin primarily in the Erzgebirge.

The GDR today produces a quarter of its gross industrial output in engineering, and a quarter of all blue- and white-collar workers are employed in this industry. As well as general and heavy engineering, metal goods and vehicle industries, the importance of shipbuilding has also increased in the GDR in recent years.[4]

Engineering is the most important export branch in the GDR, accounting for 51.2% of total exports in 1976. The engineering industry is concentrated in the three counties of Dresden, Leipzig and Karl-Marx-Stadt in Saxony, followed by Halle, Magdeburg and Erfurt. Potsdam, Suhl, Gera and East Berlin are also not without importance in the engineering industry. In shipbuilding Rostock has the leading position.

The output of the metal goods industries also serves primarily to meet the domestic demand for high-value consumer goods like refrigerators and washing-machines. In the vehicle industry only a small part of output consists of passenger-car production.

The third most important of the export industries, after engineering and consumer goods, is the chemical industry. About 12.7% of foreign trade is covered by products of the chemical industry, which today belongs to the leading, structure-determining branches of the GDR economy. The GDR chemical industry, which also includes the processing of synthetic fabrics and today produces about one-seventh of industrial output, is primarily specialised in the production of chemical raw materials and materials for further processing. In addition it supplies the population with goods made of synthetic materials, synthetic textiles, medicaments and photographic goods. Despite great expansion of the capacity of the chemical industry, it still does not display the growth-rates usual in the leading Western industrial countries. Among the Comecon countries, it takes second place after the USSR in terms of absolute volume of output. In world terms, it is in seventh place. The greatest concentration of the chemical industry is in Halle, where it accounts for more than 42% of the gross industrial output of the county and is the characteristic branch of industry. Here the districts of Bitterfeld and Merseburg with the well-known Leuna works should be mentioned. Another centre of the chemical industry is the Böhlem and Espenheim combines in the Borna district of Leipzig county. The third chemical centre in the GDR has been built up at Schwedt an der Oder, where the oil supplied via the 'Friendship' pipeline from the USSR is processed. A second pipeline brings oil to Schwedt from the port of Rostock, to which it is delivered by tanker. From Schwedt a further pipeline goes to the centre of the chemical industry in the Leuna-Bitterfeld area and takes oil products to East Berlin.

One important raw material for the chemical industry is found in the GDR in great abundance — salts, in particular potash. In absolute volume of output of potash fertilisers, the GDR occupies third place in the world after the USSR and Canada. In potash production per head the GDR comes before any other country. Two-thirds of the potash is at present produced from the Werra and South Harz deposits, where mining conditions are very favourable.

The building materials industry, because of changes in the last two decades, has typically undergone a distinct structural alteration. Traditional brick products have given way to ready-made parts and cement and concrete components. The relative neglect of production of traditional building materials (bricks, large-size building stone, cement) has led to considerable shortages. This insufficient production, and a regional distribution which does not correspond to demand, have contributed to the serious weaknesses of the GDR construction sector.

The electrical industry, which includes the production of automation equipment and control installations, is a decisive agent of growth in an industrial society. In the GDR it produces 11.2% of industrial output and is concentrated primarily in East Berlin, followed by the counties of Dresden, with the famous 'Robotron' computer works, Karl-Marx-Stadt and Erfurt. The output of this sector has increased tenfold since 1950. The technical level of some of the sector's output, primarily in the computer industry, is still below world standards; the computers produced are mostly second-generation while the West is already working on the development of fourth-generation computers.

In the precision engineering and optical industries the GDR is among the leading countries of the world — for example, it holds fifth place in typewriter production. The precision engineering and optical enterprises are concentrated in their traditional industrial area, which lies primarily in Gera, Erfurt and Suhl — one has only to think of the Carl Zeiss works in Jena. The world-famous 'Pentacon' cameras are manufactured in Dresden.

The textile and clothing industries are among the most traditional ones in the GDR. They are concentrated in the following areas, in order of economic importance: the Saxony and East Thuringia textile area in the counties of Karl-Marx-Stadt and Gera; the Oberlausitz (East Saxony) textile area in the county of Dresden; the Niederlausitz (South Brandenburg) textile area in the county of Cottbus; the west Thuringia textile area in the county of Erfurt, and the textile and clothing industry in the county of Leipzig.

The textiles produced are mainly exported to the United Kingdom and the Federal German Republic, so that only second- and third-rate textiles are available to supply the domestic population. The GDR scored a success with the discovery of an artificial fibre called 'Dederon' — the name is derived from the German version of 'GDR' ('DDR').

The food industry, with 18% of gross industrial output; light industry, with 11.3%; and the textile industry, with 7%, form the consumption-oriented branches of industry in the GDR. Since 1950 their level of output has only approximately tripled and their share of gross industrial output has declined meanwhile from 47% to 36%, thus illustrating clearly how economic planning has given priority to the production of investment goods and the development of the basic materials sector at the expense of consumer goods production. The mass demand for foodstuffs in densely populated, overcrowded regions led to the concentration of the food industry in East Berlin and the urban districts of Dresden, Rostock, Magdeburg, Halle and Leipzig. Rostock, with its fishing combine, is also the centre of the fish-processing industry. Since the foodstuffs sector had been severely neglected, investment in this industry has increased most since 1960 and has quadrupled since that time.

Agriculture

The GDR is divided into four main climatic regions: the first region, with a continental climate, includes the counties of Magdeburg, Potsdam, Frankfurt an der Oder, Halle, Cottbus and East Berlin. This zone is also reckoned to take in the eastern parts of the counties of Neubrandenburg and Erfurt as well as the northern parts of the county of Leipzig. This climatic region typically has small annual precipitation figures, combined with low average humidity and a relatively favourable annual average temperature.

The second climatic region, with a maritime climate, contains the counties of Rostock, Schwerin, part of Neubrandenburg and the northern parts of Magdeburg, Potsdam and Frankfurt-on-the-Oder. In contrast to the continental climate, precipitation figures here are higher; one-third of the annual precipitation falls in the months of June to August, and temperature variations are less marked.

The third climatic region consists of the transitional areas, the northern parts of the counties of Dresden and Gera and the southern parts of Erfurt and Leipzig: they are transitional because they lead to the climate of the German central mountains. Higher precipitation is typical, while the annual average temperature is comparable with the continental climate.

The climate of the foothills and mountains belongs to the fourth climatic region, including the counties o. Suhl and Karl-Marx-Stadt and the southern parts of Gera and Dresden, the northwestern parts of Erfurt and the Harz district of Magdeburg and Halle. This region, which contains the Harz, the lower Rhön, the Thuringian and Franconian forests, and the Elster, Erz and Elbsandstein mountains, is marked by higher annual precipitation rates, low annual average temperatures and a short growing season. This leads to restriction of the period in which field work can be undertaken and limits the choice of cultivable crops. Thus agricultural production is severely restricted in these areas.[5]

The quality of soil varies from rich loess soils to infertile sands. The high-yielding loess soil regions are primarily in the counties of Magdeburg, Halle and Leipzig. Overall, it can be said that natural conditions for agricultural production in the GDR are somewhat less favourable than in the Federal Republic. Years with relatively low precipitation on light soils are therefore bound to lead to large harvest losses.

Transport

Transport in the GDR suffers from a scarcity of funds available for building up its infrastructure. Nearly all the new building projects and extensions in the transport infrastructure have come into being for political purposes: thus the Havel canal, the only extension of the waterways network, was built in order to circumnavigate West Berlin. The outer railway ring round Berlin was constructed for the same purpose. The port of Rostock was extended in order to be independent of the ports of Hamburg and Stettin (now in Poland).

Today it consists of two modern 10-metre-deep basins on the Warnow river, half-way between the city and the sea, where the river broadens out into a kind of inland sea. The new port is to be extended to become an oil terminal by deepening the access channel. In addition, it is planned to construct a container terminal and depot. GDR ships are already carrying on a brisk container traffic with Great Britain, mostly out of Rostock but also through Hamburg. The Deutsche Seereederei line operates services from Rostock to Asia, Africa and America, mostly to the socialist countries of Vietnam and Cuba. There is of course a lively shipping traffic from Rostock to Soviet, Finnish and Norwegian ports.

Rostock is in competition with Polish ports, but to remedy this situation a GDR-Polish organisation called 'Interport' was set up at the end of 1973 to coordinate shipping and freight destined for the two countries. From Warnemünde — the sea basin down the river from Rostock — ferry services to Denmark and Sweden are being developed. Besides its principal port of Rostock, the GDR has two further seaports, Wismar and Stralsund. In 1976 the country's merchant fleet consisted of 1,211,898 gross registered tons.

Owing to destruction, dismantling and closures, the capacity of the GDR railway network was substantially restricted after the war, primarily in the areas near the Polish and Czechoslovak borders. Today only the main lines of the former (pre-Second World War) German railways in the GDR have once again been double-tracked. The 1,406 km. which are electrified, out of the total rail network of 14,298 km., are almost exclusively in the industrial region of Saxony, where construction had already begun before the war. Many lines are still not equipped with automatic safety installations. There is still a low level of comfort, which can only be improved by welding the rails.

The road network of the GDR can on the whole be described as dense, but it nevertheless shows marked regional differences. While the industrial south already possessed a road network which was adequate in terms of capacity at the end of the war, the mainly agricultural north region of the GDR has a very low road density. Hitherto major road works in the GDR have been confined almost exclusively to the maintenance and rebuilding of the existing network of 1,491 km. of *Autobahn*, 11,000 km. of trunk and 33,000 km. of main roads, and 57,000 km. of local roads. Construction of an *Autobahn* from Berlin to Rostock is planned. The Federal Republic is interested in the building of an *Autobahn* from Hamburg to Berlin, and would be willing to share in its financing.

In 1945 the then Soviet occupation zone already had a well-developed waterway system at its disposal, which today runs to 2,538 km. Its importance was substantially reduced when the Elbe and Oder rivers became frontiers of the GDR and when Berlin assumed its present status. Neither the industrial region of Saxony nor the centres of brown coal mining are served by adequate waterways. There have been many plans to build a north-south canal.

As regards urban transport, the cities of Leipzig, Dresden, Halle, Magdeburg and Rostock either already have a rapid rail network or are building such a system. Public urban transport in the GDR still largely takes the form of trams.

In air transport, Schönefeld was expanded into a major international airport, which also has rail and motorway connections. Leipzig airport is important for traffic to and from the many trade fairs in the city, as is Barth airport on the Baltic for holiday traffic. In Saxony there are flights to the newly extended airport at Dresden, and in Thuringia to Erfurt. In 1976 the GDR airline Interflug carried more than 1.1 million passengers.[6]

2
History

The Allies agreed during the war that in order to ensure the destruction of National Socialism in Germany, the defeated country should be subjected to a strict occupation regime. For this purpose the territory of the former German *Reich* was to be divided: first into three and later, with the participation of France, into four occupation zones and a special area of Greater Berlin, with one zone allocated to each of the Allies. Plans for the dismemberment of Germany into different component states were discussed at inter-Allied conferences from 1941 onwards, but at the beginning of 1945 they were dropped at the instigation of the USSR.

The Potsdam Agreement of 1945 confirmed the division of Germany into occupation zones and the assumption of supreme state power in Germany by the four occupying powers, who created the necessary institutions and laid down the principles for a uniform treatment of the whole of Germany. The repeated accusations from the Eastern side of failure by the West to fulfil the Potsdam resolutions are based primarily on a one-sided interpretation of the Potsdam Agreement by the GDR and the USSR.

Ultimately the disagreement over who did or did not fulfil the Potsdam Agreement, or who violated it first and who more seriously, is not the issue. The problem, as has rightly been pointed out, lies much deeper, namely in the imprecise formulations of the Potsdam Agreement, to which the Allies agreed as a compromise. The central concepts in the Agreement, like the terms 'democratic' and 'peaceful', are ambiguous and subject to different intepretations. Even Eastern specialists in international law concede that the question of the interpretation of the concept of democracy is not as unequivocal as is always maintained in their countries' official policies.

It is fairly clear that the demilitarisation of Germany stipulated in the Potsdam Agreement was violated by the Soviet side. As early as the middle of 1946, military arrangements were made in the Soviet Occupation Zone (SBZ), followed in 1948 by the build-up of regular troops disguised as 'People's Police in Barracks', which soon developed into an operational fighting force. The principle established at Potsdam whereby the whole of Germany should be treated as one economic unit, notwithstanding its division into zones, was infringed in a decisive respect at P̶ ̶ ̶t̶self. Since the Soviet Union pressed for the satisfactic̶ ̶ ̶rations demands predominantly from its own zon̶ ̶the German economy — in respect of the payment ̶ was abandoned. The three Western occupation po̶ cover their reparations demands from their zones. In add̶ declared themselves ready to hand over 25% of the ind̶ equipment in the Western zones which was no longer necessary f̶ the post-war German economy to the Soviet Union as compensation for the fact that the Soviet zone only contained a small part of German industrial capacity. In return, the Soviet Union undertook to supply foodstuffs and other commodities from its occupation zone in payment for 15% of this 25%. According to Western calculations the total reparations taken from the SBZ/GDR by the Soviet Union up to 1953 amounted to $15.8 mlrd. The total loss was estimated at 40-45% of the industrial capacity of that part of Germany in 1936, more than the benefit given to West Germany by Marshall Aid.

The question of Soviet counterpayments for the reparations received from the Western occupation zones sparked off a conflict between East and West in the Four-Power Administration of Germany. This conflict hampered cooperation in the Control Commission still more, and finally led to the fusion of the American and British zones into the Bi-Zone and ultimately, after the merger with the French zone, to the preparation of a West German state. At a session of the Allied Control Commission on 20 March 1948 in Berlin, the Soviet commander in the SBZ, Marshal Sokolovsky, requested information on the decisions taken shortly before at the London Conference of the Western powers, the subject of which had been the formation of a West German state, the eventual Federal Republic of Germany. The Western powers refused, and the Russian walked out of the Control Commission. This step by the Soviet Union finally broke up the joint four-power government of Germany. In view of the increasing differences beween the USSR and the Western Allies, this was no great surprise to anyone.

In 1948, after the introduction of the new West German currency and in response to the situation which had arisen after the collapse of the joint four-power government, Moscow began the year-long blockade of the access routes to West Berlin. This blockade was intended to exert pressure on the Western powers to compel them to abandon their plans for the establishment of a separate West German state. Thanks to the Allied airlift and the discipline of the West Berliners, the blockade failed.

With his famous words 'Hitlers come and go but the German people remain', Stalin had already sought to distinguish between

National Socialism and the German people during the last months of the war. Like the Western powers (apart from French policy on Germany before 1948), the Soviet Union wanted to preserve the unity of Germany, but in the form of a people's democracy. Consequently, the Western plans to establish a separate West German state must have been a thorn in Stalin's flesh.

Foundation of parties

Even before the beginning of the Potsdam Conference, the USSR was the first of the occupying powers to start on the reactivation of political life in Germany, with the foundation of anti-fascist democratic parties and free trade unions, on the basis of the famous Order No. 2 of 10 June 1945 issued by the Soviet Military Administration in Germany. The aims of Soviet policy towards Germany, which was principally carried out by the Ulbricht group, were revealed by the fact that on the day following the issue of the Soviet order, 11 June 1945, the Communist Party of Germany (KPD) came out with a call to the German people in which it referred to the responsibility and guilt of Germany in the general catastrophe of the Second World War and drew conclusions for the future political development of Germany. In this appeal the KPD laid the guilt and the responsibility for the war and its consequences not only on Hitler and National Socialism but on the German people. It said:

Not only Hitler is guilty of the crimes which were committed against humanity, but the 10 million Germans who voted for Hitler in free elections in 1932, although we communists warned that 'a vote for Hitler is a vote for war', bear their share of guilt.

The KPD demanded a thorough settling of accounts with the National Socialist past, confiscation of National Socialist property, elimination of large-scale ownership of land, introduction of a democratic participatory administration, the establishment of a new school system and free election of enterprise representatives. In this first phase of its policy, the KPD rejected deliberate Sovietisation of Germany. On the contrary:

We are of the opinion that it would be wrong to force the Soviet system on Germany, since this does not correspond to the present conditions of development in Germany. We are rather of the opinion that the crucial interests of the German people in the present situation prescribe a different path for Germany, the path of construction of an anti-fascist, democratic regime, a parliamentary democratic republic with all democratic rights and freedoms for the people.

The policy of the KPD was directed throughout towards the whole of Germany in order that it should be able to share actively in shaping the political situation, and because 'it would be very wrong to lead the struggle for the immediate construction of socialism' until proletarian class consciousness had recovered after the period of National Socialism. Therefore the policy of the KPD was aimed initially at the 'creation of a block of anti-fascist, democratic parties', without immediate pressure for organisational unification with the Socialist Party of Germany (SPD).[7]

In order to be able to create this block the foundation of other political parties in the SBZ was necessary. On 15 June 1945 the SPD published a foundation appeal, on 26 June 1945 the Christian-Democratic Union (CDU) and on 15 July 1945 the Liberal-Democratic Party (LDPD) followed suit. The KPD proposal for united action by all democratic parties was taken up by the SPD:

We are ready and resolved to cooperate in this with all like-minded people and parties. We warmly welcome the appeal of the Central Committee of the Communist Party of Germany of 11 June 1945 which correctly declares that the path of reconstruction is dependent on the present development conditions in Germany and that the crucial interests of the German people in the present situation require the establishment of an anti-fascist democratic regime and a parliamentary democratic republic with all democratic rights and freedoms for the people.[8]

Both the other parties proceeded on the basis of a similar assessment of the situation. This is not surprising in view of the pressure of the Soviet occupying power, and the parties had no alternative to close cooperation. On 19 June 1945 a joint KPD and SPD working committee was formed, which among other things was to discuss the implementation of joint arrangements and the 'classification of ideological questions'. On 14 July 1945 the united front of anti-fascist democratic parties proposed by the KPD was formed, to which five representatives each of the KPD, SPD, CDU and LDPD belonged.

The merger of the two workers' parties into a united party was strictly rejected by the KPD leadership until the autumn of 1945. The then chairman of the KPD, Wilhelm Pieck, declared on 19 July 1945:

We know that the pressure for this unity is very great, especially in the working class. But today the time to create this united party has not yet come because there must first be a great spiritual revolution in the working class in order to create a firm foundation for this united party.[9]

The ideological and organisational preparations had first to be made for a merger of the KPD with the SPD. Initially the KPD was afraid most of all of becoming a minority *vis-à-vis* the SPD members. In the SPD too there was great opposition to a merger, because it was against the close contacts which the KPD maintained with the Soviet Military Administration.

Around the turn of the year 1945-6 the demand for unification of the two parties was stepped up by the KPD leadership, but rejected by the majority of SPD members; in the SPD leadership in the SBZ it was controversial and was strongly resisted by Kurt Schumacher. At the joint conference of the KPD and SPD central committees on 20 and 21 December 1945, the draft of a declaration on the principles and aims of a united socialist party was discussed, which was supposed to establish agreement on a programme. A joint resolution stated:

The united party is to be autonomous and independent. Its task, its policy and its tactics are to be developed in accordance with the interests of the German working people and the special conditions of Germany. Both in the implementation of the minimum programme and of the maximum programme it is to pursue its own path, based on the particular features of the development of our people.

(The minimum programme aimed at completing the restoration of democracy, the maximum programme at the implementation of socialism.)

The particular German road to socialism was presented by the KPD theorist Anton Ackermann in February 1946 in his famous essay 'Is there a particular German road to socialism?', in which he stressed that in Germany it was possible to pursue a 'relatively peaceful road' to socialism,

since, because of special circumstances, the bourgeoisie does not have control of the military and bureaucratic apparatus of state power, which otherwise enables it to counter the proletariat's demand for power with civil war and terrorist suppression of the proletarian-socialist movement.[10]

Against the background of this particular German road to socialism, the KPD and the SPD convened separate party congresses in Berlin on 19-20 April 1946, which were followed on 21 and 22 April by the unification congress, at which the merger of the two parties was completed with the symbolic handshake between the KPD chairman Wilhelm Pieck and the chairman of the SPD in the Eastern zone, Otto Grotewohl, which still adorns the party badge of every SED member today. In the Western zones the unification of the two large workers' parties was rejected by the SPD. In Berlin too the two parties did not merge, since a poll of SPD members in the three Western sectors of the city, which took place on 30 March 1946 with the support of the Western powers, resulted in 82% voting against the unification of the SPD with the KPD.

Initially party bodies in the SED consisted of equal numbers of former KPD and former SPD members. But from 1947 onwards the SED developed more and more into a Marxist-Leninist cadre party.

More and more party bodies were filled with former KPD members at the expense of former SPD members. At the first party conference of the SED on 28 January 1949, it was declared quite clearly a 'new type of party'. In one resolution the conference stated:

Party discussion has also made it clear that we are on the way to a new style of party, a party fighting for Marxism-Leninism ... The Marxist-Leninist party is based on the principle of democratic centralism. This means strict adherence to the principle of election of administrations and functionaries and the accountability of those elected to the members. This intra-party democracy is the basis of the strict party discipline which stems from the socialist consciousness of the members. Party resolutions apply to all members without exception, especially those actively involved in parliaments, governments, administrative organs and the administrative bodies of the mass organisations ... The toleration of fractions and groupings within the party is incompatible with its Marxist-Leninist character.[11]

This Bolshevisation of the SED took place as part of a reinforced policy of coordination within the Eastern bloc as a consequence of the exclusion of Yugoslavia from the Cominform. All attempts 'to make the SED into an opportunist party of the Western type' were repulsed, and the signal was given for an implacable fight against 'social democracy'. The particular road to socialism put forward by Ackermann was rejected as 'wrong theory'.

Simultaneously with the Bolshevisation of the SED, two further political parties were founded: the National-Democratic Party of Germany (NDPD) on 25 May 1948 and the Democratic Peasant Party of Germany (DBD) on 25 April 1948. According to its own declaration, the NDPD is a party for

handicraftsmen and retail traders, entrepreneurs and members of the intelligentsia and also former officers and professional soldiers in the former imperialist army and one-time members of the former NSDAP [Nazi] who have broken with their past and have become democrats and patriots.[12]

In contrast to the Soviet Union, Hungary and Romania, various parties continue to exist or were allowed again in the GDR. Their existence was intended to simulate political pluralism in the eyes of the West. In addition, the various parties in the GDR have the task of representing the interests of the SED *vis-à-vis* their members, who belong to particular social groups and strata or creeds, and not infrequently endeavour to avoid SED membership by entry into these 'bourgeois' parties. In this way the SED obtains a better opportunity to mould itself as a communist cadre party. And finally, during the phase of the SED's all-Germany policy in the post-war years, the bourgeois parties in the GDR exercised limited bridge-building functions, establishing contacts with their West German sister-parties.

On 14 July 1945 the united front of the 'anti-fascist democratic block' was officially constituted. The communiqué stated:

The representatives of the four parties, mutually recognising their independence, resolved upon the formation of a firm united front of anti-fascist democratic parties, in order with their united strength to solve the great problems ahead. Thus a new leaf was turned in the history of Germany.[13]

Even the bourgeois parties found no grounds for refusal in the five points of the block's programme: cooperation in purging Germany of the remnants of Hitlerism, reconstruction of the country and the economy, creation of full legal security, assurance of freedom of thought, and regaining a relationship of confidence with all peoples.

The KPD, and subsequently the SED in the SBZ of 1945-9, had won power neither in a real revolutionary manner nor by peaceful means through gaining a majority in a parliamentary election. With the support of the Soviet Military Administration it made use of the instrument of block politics in the framework of a united front of all parties of the anti-fascist democratic block. While the Eastern CDU was already opposing the policies of the KPD-SED in 1945, the year of its foundation, for which it twice had to pay with the exclusion of its leadership (Hermes and Schreiber were removed because of their opposition to the methods used in carrying out the land reform in December 1945, Kaiser and Lemmer because of their critical attitude to the people's congress movement in November 1947), the LDPD only developed a comparable opposition attitude three years later. The LDPD evidently took the view — according to various investigations — that the relations existing at that time were to be regarded as transitional and that extensive cooperation with the SED was indicated. The LDPD had stressed what it shared in common with the SED, without approving the latter's ultimate aim. One could go 'a good stretch of road together' with Marxism. The then LDPD leaders had failed to understand the dynamic revolutionary nature of Marxism-Leninism and saw in communism only another variety of democratic politics. The difference consisted only in method, not in essence.

According to historical studies of the period the mistake of the two bourgeois parties, the LDPD and the CDU, was that from the beginning they had omitted to establish statutory responsibilities and procedures in the united block against a possible misuse of power.

The representatives of the bourgeois parties in the SBZ did not by any means silently approve the concept of a united front under the leadership of the SED, but in the political situation of the time, above all in view of the Soviet presence, there was nothing else left

for them but to agree to the programme of an anti-fascist democratic block developed by the SED. After the foundation of the
mass organisations, they too were incorporated into the Democratic
Block of Parties and Mass Organisations, among other things in
order to reduce the influence of the two bourgeois parties, the CDU
and LDPD. The Union of Free German Trade Unions (FDGB) was
founded on 15 June 1945, the German Cultural Union likewise in
1945, the Free German Youth (FDJ) on 7 March 1946 and the
Democratic Women's Union of Germany (DFD) on 8 March 1947.

Domestic political reform programme

The domestic policy programme of the SED in the first years after
the war included fundamental structural changes like the land,
economic and educational reforms. The land reform was started as
early as September 1945 in Saxony. In accordance with the decree
on confiscation without compensation of all land holdings in excess
of 100 hectares, not only was every such holding confiscated but
also smaller holdings belonging to those who could be branded as
Nazis or militarists. The confiscated land was allotted to new
peasants in farms of from 2.5 to 10 hectares of arable land.

Parallel to the confiscation of land, in October 1945 the Soviet
Military Administration carried out the confiscation of the property
of the German *Reich*, the state of Prussia, the NSDAP and large
industrial, mining and trading firms. 'Almost half the industrial
capacity of the SBZ passed to the provinces or counties and cities.'
The confiscated firms were operated as nationalised enterprises
(VEB). The Soviets themselves took over 25% of the confiscated
industrial property, and for this purpose founded special Soviet
joint stock companies (SAG) which existed until 1953 and had a
considerable influence on the economic development of the SBZ
and the subsequent GDR. The removal of the means of production
from private hands to the state laid the foundations for the
establishment of a socialist centrally administered economy, typical
of all the East European countries today.

An equally thoroughgoing reform was carried out in the school
and training system. The May 1946 'Law on the democratisation of
the German school' proclaimed the 'democratic unity school'. This
school provided for all children to attend the same basic school for
eight years, where they would be educated according to Marxist-
Leninist ideology to be loyal citizens of the GDR in the sense of
socialist internationalism (see chapter 5).

At the same time as the fifth session of the Conference of
Foreign Ministers of the four victorious powers was held in London
(from 25 November to 15 December), in an atmosphere of tension
resulting from the escalation of the cold war, to discuss the

preparation of a German peace treaty and the restoration of the political unity of Germany, the SED convened the first 'German People's Congress for Unity and a Just Peace'. This was attended by 2,000 delegates from the whole of Germany under the leadership of the SED. This People's Congress addressed a resolution to the foreign ministers meeting in London, advocating a peace on the basis of the Yalta and Potsdam conferences. The second People's Congress met on the centenary of the 1848 Revolution in March 1948 with the slogan 'From the Paulskirche [where the 1848 assembly met at Frankfurt-am-Main] to the People's Congress' and declared itself in favour of the creation of an anti-fascist democracy in the whole of Germany. This People's Congress saw itself as the 'completion and conclusion of the trend initiated in Germany in 1848', and elected a 'German People's Council' as a deliberative and decision-making organ to act between sessions of the People's Congress and to conduct 'the struggle for the unity of Germany and for a just peace treaty'. On 19 March 1949 this German People's Council passed a draft, which had been prepared by the SED in 1946 and approved by the 1948 People's Congress, for a constitution of a German Democratic Republic, with elections to the third People's Congress based on the united list of parties and mass organisations combined in the democratic block. The individual parties and mass organisations within this block were allocated specified quotas of votes or delegates before the election.

The third People's Congress in May 1949 was attended by 1,600 delegates from the SBZ and 616 from West Germany. This Congress confirmed once again the draft constitution of a German Democratic Republic which has already been mentioned, and set up a new People's Council consisting of 400 members. After the foundation of the Federal Republic of Germany, the first elections to the *Bundestag* and the formation of the first Federal German government on 7 October 1949, this new People's Council decided on the foundation of the German Democratic Republic.

The SED sought to achieve the legitimation of its power in elections. For this purpose the first local elections in the SBZ took place in September 1946, when the SED gained overall somewhat more than 50% of the votes. Yet it must be noted that the bourgeois parties in the Democratic Block had been hampered and discriminated against in the preparations for the elections by the Soviet occupying power. Clause 28 of the Election Regulations of 28 June 1946, which were endorsed by the Soviet Military Administration (SMA), meant that nominations for candidates could only be put forward by local delegations of the parties and 'anti-fascist democratic organisations' which had been registered with the SMA. Whilst the SED was accepted and registered in all the constituencies and in consequence could nominate candidates everywhere, the non-Communist parties were at a considerable disadvantage. In only a fraction of the constituencies of the SBZ did the local groups of the CDU and LDPD gain registration.

Considering there were over 4,200 local groups of the CDU and over 2,200 of the LDPD in the Soviet Zone these two parties were refused a good half of their applications for registration. Although selection committees had been elected and lists of members were submitted, registration was either indefinitely postponed or refused on tenuous grounds. Thus in Saxony, from 1-15 August, 531 new local groups of the SED were registered, whilst the total registered between 1-27 August for the CDU was 164 and for the LDPD 194.

In addition to these serious set-backs to the non-communist parties, there was also the fact that the SED received numerous favours from the SMA. The SED had over 800 tonnes of paper for election purposes placed at its disposal, whereas the CDU and LDPD together received a mere 9 tonnes. Moreover, the daily newspaper, the 'Tägliche Rundschau', organ of the SMA, carried out a programme of clearly one-sided election propaganda for the SED. SED newspapers appeared in editions of millions, whilst the meagre CDU and LDPD newspapers in the Soviet Zone and the Soviet sector of Berlin only managed to print one edition of a few hundred thousand; furthermore, they were not produced daily, but, at most, twice a week.

During the election campaign itself, numerous posters and broadsheets of the CDU and LDPD were outlawed by the local SMA; approval for other posters and broad-sheets was delayed so long that their effective use was destroyed. Some were even altered by the local SMA. Furthermore, as a result of the Soviet censure, the non-communist parties were unable to present their arguments effectively in the election campaign. Permission to hold a large number of proposed gatherings was either not granted or otherwise continually deferred. The SMA also blocked certain party speakers or demanded that the speech be officially approved before being delivered. Non-Communist speakers were frequently harassed following election speeches.

In the district and provincial elections, which were first held in the SBZ on 20 October 1946, the SED was indeed victorious in all five provinces, but with a share of the vote below 50%. As an example of the possible voting pattern of the population of the SBZ in genuinely free elections — the elections mentioned hitherto can be considered only relatively free — we can look at the elections held in Greater Berlin on 20 October 1946. In these elections for the Berlin city assembly the shares of the vote in East Berlin were SED 29.8%, SPD 43.6%, CDU 18.7% and LDPD 7.9%.

According to GDR history books the collapse of the conference of prime ministers of the German provinces in Munich in June 1947

forms the crucial turning-point on the road to the division of
Germany. This conference, to which the Bavarian prime minister
Ehard had issued the invitations, was intended to discuss joint
measures to alleviate the enormous economic distress in Germany.
Not only were the five prime ministers from the SBZ late in arriving
in Munich, but they also demanded that the conference discuss the
question of German unity as the first item on the agenda. Since the
West German prime ministers had received instructions from the
three Western occupation powers not to discuss the question of the
unity of Germany at this conference, a compromise was sought but
without success, so the five prime ministers from the SBZ left
prematurely. They were now able to argue that their Western
counterparts were not prepared to discuss the central problem of
the creation of a unified German state. In this, as in a number of
other cases such as the currency reform and the foundation of the
Federal Republic of Germany, the GDR can always point to the
fact that the first formal steps towards the formation of a partial
German state were taken by the West German or Western side,
although these were countermeasures to the division which had
already been brought about in practice by the SBZ or GDR.

The GDR as a new German state was designated as illegitimate
by the Adenauer government since it had not been democratically
legitimated by its own population through free parliamentary
elections. Consequently Adenauer claimed that according to the
principles of natural law, the Federal Republic of Germany alone
represented the interests of the whole German people. The GDR
could claim no right to a voice in questions which affected the
whole of Germany, as all these questions were the responsibility of
the four victorious powers.

The first GDR government under the premiership of Grotewohl,
who originated from the SPD, and with the SED chairman Pieck as
President, regarded itself as the first independent government of
the German people, democratically elected. However, democracy
in this case does not mean our Western or, as they would say in the
GDR, bourgeois concept of democracy, but socialist democracy.
Socialist democracy, according to the GDR's own interpretation, is
the exercise of political power by the working masses of the people,
led by the working class and its Marxist-Leninist party, which
vanquishes and abolishes formal bourgeois democracy with the
establishment of the dictatorship of the proletariat. Socialist democracy requires the working class to fulfil its leading role in society,
and that the principal means of production should be in social
ownership. The leading role of the working class is the political
foundation of socialist democracy; the socialist social ownership of
the principal means of production is its economic foundation.[14]

Rigidified fronts

The two German states were founded during the first high point of the Cold War. The Berlin Blockade of 1948-9 and the outbreak of the Korean War a year later made the threat of the worldwide Cold War between the two great powers clear. Each of the two powers made great efforts to incorporate the part of Germany which it controlled, and had now formed into a state, firmly into its own respective sphere of dominion. The reduction of the level of GDR reparations to the USSR in May 1950 and the treaty of 6 June 1950 between the GDR and Poland 'on the designation of the established and existing German-Polish state frontier on the Oder and the Lausitz Neisse' are stages in the course of complete integration of the GDR into the Eastern block. The admission of the GDR into the Council for Mutual Economic Assistance (Comecon) on 29 September 1950 and its participation in the Warsaw Pact — of which the GDR was one of the founder-members on 14 May 1955 — formally concluded this process of integration.

The Cold War, with its rigidified fronts of East-West antagonism, also impeded every tentative solution of the German question. On 30 November 1950 the then Prime Minister of the GDR, Otto Grotewohl, proposed in a letter the formation of an 'all-German constitutive council composed of a parity of representatives of East and West Germany, which should prepare for the formation of an all-German, sovereign, democratic and peace-loving provisional government'. This letter, and subsequent similar proposals, failed to gain a hearing from the Federal government because the GDR would not accept free, universal, equal, secret and direct elections in both parts of Germany as a precondition for the formation of such an all-German organ. This series of efforts by the GDR concerning the whole of Germany also includes a letter from President Wilhelm Pieck to the Federal President Theodor Heuss on 2 November 1951, which raised the question of the way to convene an all-German government. In his answer to Pieck, Heuss said, among other things:

Your assessment of the present situation and the tone in which you express it must make the possibility of discussions you advocate questionable from the beginning. Your polemics against the Federal government and the *Bundestag* are such as to undermine the seriousness of your proposal. An exchange of views at this level is basically useless and would only become a source of new disappointments.[15]

As a result, the GDR opposed the formation of a United Nations Commission for Germany. It refused the members of the commission entry to East Berlin and the GDR. In its report of 30 April 1952 the Commission stated:

Whilst the commission was able to fulfil its preparatory task in the Federal
Republic of German and in the Western sector of Berlin, it has not hitherto
been able to communicate even in writing with the authorities in the Soviet
zone of Germany and in the Eastern sector of Berlin. It was consequently
not possible for the commission to make the arrangements with the
authorities concerned in the Soviet zone of Germany or in the Eastern
sector of Berlin, which it regards as necessary to enable it to discharge its
duties in accordance with its commission.[16]

Domestically, the formal ending of denazification on 26 February
1948 and the law on the remission of sanctions and the granting of
rights of citizenship of 11 November 1949 concluded the denazification imposed by the Potsdam Agreement. On 7 January 1950 the
secretariat of the German People's Council resolved to rename
itself the secretariat of the National Front of Democratic Germany.
The National Front, which comprises the parties and mass organisations of the 'anti-fascist democratic block' and non-party members,
was founded on 7 October 1949. From the expanded presidium of
the People's Council, the National Council was formed on 3
February 1950 as the leading organ of the National Front. The
programme of the National Front decided by the National Council
on 15 February 1950 described the foundation of the GDR as a
turning-point for the whole of Germany. The crucial task was said
to be the 'mobilisation and organisation of the Germans for the
liberation of Germany from the presence and machinations of the
Anglo-American imperialists'. A prerequisite for the successful
struggle was 'firm, indestructible friendship with the Soviet Union'.
All parties and mass organisations, and all citizens who did not
belong to any party or mass organisation, were called upon to work
together in the National Front. One of the chief tasks of the
National Front was declared to be the fulfilment and overfulfilment of national economic plans.

Consolidation

As a stage in the 'transition from capitalism to socialism', the
second party conference of the SED in 1952 decided on 'the
planned construction of the basis of socialism'. As a sign of its
consolidation of power, the SED further transformed itself into a
'real Marxist-Leninist fighting party', on account of which the first
statute, adopted in 1946, was superseded by a second statute
adopted at the III Party Congress in 1950. The ideological struggle
against 'social democracy' in the party and the trade unions also
helped to strengthen its power. At the first elections to the National
Assembly in the GDR in 1950, the SED succeeded in pushing
through its united list against the initial opposition of the Eastern
CDU and the LDPD.

Following the decision to construct socialism, a law was passed by the National Assembly in July 1952 'on the further democratisation of the structure and mode of operation of state organs in the provinces', which abolished the five provinces of Mecklenburg, Brandenburg, Saxony-Anhalt, Saxony and Thuringia and replaced them by the centralised system of fifteen counties.

After the conclusion of the 1949-50 two-year plan, the SED adopted at its III Congress, held on 20-24 July 1950, the principles for the first GDR five-year plan for 1951-5. At the end of 1949 the nationalised and cooperative sector of the GDR economy already produced more than half of the gross social product and some two-thirds of the GDR's industrial output. The complete switch-over of the economy to the Soviet planned economic system took place after the collapse of the SED initiatives concerning Germany as a whole in 1950 and 1951 and the failure of the 1952 Soviet note on Germany. The new five-year plan envisaged the acceleration of economic development.

A rigorous policy on norms was intended to achieve economic successes, but led in fact to differences of opinion within the SED Politburo and growing dissatisfaction among the population. The increasing socialist transformation of the economy had led to serious supply difficulties in the autumn of 1952. The drastic raising of labour norms with unchanged wages and the shock to the Stalinist leading circles in the GDR of the death of Stalin on 5 March 1953 heralded developments which escalated to the uprising of 17 June 1953. The announcement of the 'New Course' on 9 June 1953 was no longer enough to appease the discontent of the population. The spontaneous strikes and workers' demonstrations in various cities in the GDR on 16 and 17 June 1953 no longer stopped at demands concerned with labour and wages policies but were soon calling for a general political and social revolution. This uprising, which was only put down with the help of Soviet tanks, was followed by a wave of arrests. In former Nazi prisons, those arrested were tortured by SS methods until they confessed themselves guilty of crimes which they had never committed. By means of show trials the SED sought to substantiate its version of the uprising, according to which a counterrevolution and an attempted fascist putsch had occurred on 17 June, directed from West Berlin by West German and American politicians and secret service circles.

At internal party discussions, a certain alienation between party and population was admitted, which had led to 'the destruction of the correct relations between the party and the working masses and to the use of administrative methods in place of widespread and patient instruction among the masses'. At the fifteenth session of the SED Central Committee on 26 July 1953, the opposition in the

Politburo — the Minister for State Security, Wilhelm Zaisser, and the chief editor of *Neues Deutschland*, Rudolf Herrnstadt — were removed from office.

After the death of Stalin the SED found itself in a transitional situation in which it had to take into account the new tendencies in the USSR, as well as considering how to react to Adenauer's policy, which was integrating the Federal Republic of Germany more and more firmly into the Western community. The SED used national arguments to attack the prospective foundation of the European Economic Community. The document adopted by the IV Party Congress in 1954, entitled 'The Way to the Solution of the Vital Question of the German Nation', was intended, by holding out the prospect of eventual reunification, to restrain the Federal Republic from entering the West European defence community. As a reaction to the entry of the Federal Republic into NATO, the USSR concluded a treaty with the GDR on 20 September 1955 by which the second German state attained its full sovereignty and thus made the existence of the two states a political fact which could not be overlooked.

The GDR's German policy in those years was concentrated in the plan put forward in 1959 by Walter Ulbricht for a confederation of the two German states, to which the USSR fully agreed. Starting from the existence of the two German states, reunification, in the Soviet view, was only possible 'by way of negotiations and agreement between the two German states' (Khrushchev). The same line was followed by the Soviet Berlin ultimatum of 1958, the aim of which was to constitute West Berlin as an independent Free City.

Domestically, this period is described in the GDR as the phase of the 'victory of socialist production relations'. This victory was achieved in various sectors in several stages. Directly after the XX Congress of the CPSU, at which Khrushchev made his famous destalinisation speech, the third SED party conference was convened in the spring of 1956. The task was posed of 'demonstrating to all people the superiority of the socialist economic system of our republic and its advantages compared with capitalist West Germany'. This party resolution was put into effect in the shape of the second five-year plan for 1956-60, a new feature of which was 'that its principal indicators were coordinated and harmonised with the long-term economic plans of the Soviet Union and the other socialist countries'. Under this plan the state sector in industry, agriculture and trade was to increase. A considerable rise in the standard of living was also envisaged.

In the fields of culture and ideology 'socialist revolutions' were carried out, and various constitutional reforms were supposed to bring about 'a development and deepening of socialist democracy'.

Since, as a consequence of the GDR's ideological position-finding, the political and economic foundations of socialism had in essence been built in the years 1949 to 1955, it was now a matter of bringing 'the victory of socialist production relations' into all spheres of the national economy. This was gradually achieved in the various economic sectors. The first wave of collectivisation of agriculture, which had followed the 1952 decision to build socialism in the GDR, was partly continued in 1957. Under the seven-year plan the third wave of collectivisation took place in the summer of 1959 and was concluded a year later after compulsion had been resorted to.

The first area in which the socialist sector was extended was industry. The confiscation of key industries in the years 1945 to 1949 had already brought two-thirds of the GDR's industrial production into state ownership. After 1955 the remaining enterprises in private hands were also to be gradually socialised. For this purpose the formation of semi-state enterprises was initiated, through the introduction of state participation. For handicrafts and the retail trade, the formation of producers' cooperatives was pushed ahead; this step too was not taken for economic reasons, but served to integrate those groups of the population into the socialist state and social system, after the 'construction of the foundations of socialism' had again been proclaimed at the V Congress of the SED (10-16 July 1958).

In the political field measures were taken, through changes in the state apparatus, towards the further consolidation of the socialist system. In accordance with the principles of historical materialism, the state apparatus had to be functionally adapted to the changes which had meanwhile occurred in social and economic relations. For this reason the Chamber of Provinces was abolished and in place of the State President, the State Council was introduced. This period also saw the passing of the law of 18 January 1956 on the creation of the National People's Army (NVA) and the Ministry of National Defence, and of a new Labour Code on 12 April 1961.

The development of the country's own defence system was the natural consequence of the GDR's entry into the Warsaw Pact in 1955. Basically it was only necessary to transfer the 'People's Police in Barracks', which had already existed for several years, into the NVA and to expand it further. The first Minister of Defence was Willi Stoph, later Prime Minister. The GDR's defence system was completed by the SED fighting groups which the party had caused to be formed in all enterprises after the uprising of 17 June 1953. In the words of the SED Central Committee statement of November 1956, the enterprise fighting groups were to fulfil their tasks in the defence of the country 'jointly with the German People's Police and, when necessary, with units of the National

People's Army'. This first happened on a large scale when the Berlin wall was built on 13 August 1961.

The economic and social policy measures we have described led to a rapid increase in the number of refugees from the GDR to the Federal Republic. In 1960 200,000 had left the GDR, and between 1 January and 13 August 1961, the number of citizens who fled from the GDR to the Federal Republic, mostly by way of West Berlin, was 159,630. It was clear that the GDR could not accept this high rate of emigration indefinitely, the more so since the proportion of young and specialist workers among the refugees was particularly high. Thus countermeasures were anticipated.

Both the Soviet leadership and NATO were concerned with this problem. In the GDR rumours circulated about a wall to be built round Berlin, which in turn led to a further rise in the number of refugees. In July 1961 alone 30,000 GDR citizens fled. At an international press conference on 15 June 1961 Walter Ulbricht denied that a wall was to be built in Berlin:

As I understand your question, there are people in West Germany who want us to mobilise the building workers of the capital of the GDR to erect a wall. I am not aware that any such intention exists. The building workers of our capital city are principally occupied in the construction of housing and their labour is fully employed in this way. No one has the intention of erecting a wall.

In the first days of August 1,000 to 2,000 people fled from the GDR to West Berlin daily, and on 12 August 1961 the GDR Council of Ministers took a decision which it had previously agreed with the other Warsaw Pact states. This decision comprised stepping up the guarding of the GDR's western border and erecting a wall between the GDR and both East Berlin and West Berlin. In his *Kurze Geschichte der DDR* ('Short History of the GDR') the GDR historian Stefan Doernberg writes:

Early in the morning of 13 August 1961, a Sunday, the armed forces of the GDR, together with the fighting groups of the Berlin workers, took under control the whole of the hitherto open border with West Berlin and thus damped down a smouldering fire of war. The GDR Council of Ministers passed the following resolution: 'In order to forestall the hostile activity of the revanchist and military forces of West Germany and West Berlin, control over the borders of the GDR, including the border with the Western sector of Greater Berlin, has been introduced, such as is usual on the borders of every sovereign state.'[17]

Doernberg's comparison of West Berlin with a 'fire of war', and claim that the building of the wall served the maintenance of peace (this justification for it is often advanced by the GDR), would indicate, unless these assertions are dismissed as pure propaganda, that the alternative plans of the GDR and the Warsaw Pact must have involved a larger military operation to come to grips with the refugee problem.

The building of the wall in 1961, as an important turning-point in post-war German history, is called by Doernberg 'the beginning of a new chapter in the history of the GDR'. One West German historian, Ernst Deuerlein, takes the following position:

The measures of 13 August 1961, by separating and integrating East Berlin, represent the consummation of the division of Germany. They were interpreted not as the conclusion but as an intermediate stage in a trend of development. By removing the possibility of flight to West Berlin they compelled the population of East Germany to remain, even when faced with political or personal difficulties. The inhabitants of the GDR had to make the best they could of the existing régime.[18]

On the GDR's border with the Federal Republic of Germany, over 433 km. of mines were laid and 291 km. of automatic spring guns were installed. Since the building of the wall, 171 people have been killed in attempts to escape into Berlin and along the GDR's border with the Federal Republic. Some 5,000-6,000 GDR citizens succeed in escaping each year. In 1976 a further 9,016 received permission from the state to emigrate to the Federal Republic.

The building of the wall, although a severe shock which hit many hard, contributed to the stabilisation of the GDR. The other possibility — namely, reducing the number of refugees by making the country so attractive that there was no longer any incentive for flight — was for various political reasons out of the question for the GDR.

On the road to the socialist 'society of achievement'

The GDR drew various political and ideological conclusions from the building of the wall. The 'National Document', published by the National Council of the National Front of Democratic Germany in May 1962, served as a basis for legitimation of the definitive separation between the GDR and the Federal Republic. This document, the precise title of which was *Die geschichtliche Aufgabe der DDR und die Zukunft Deutschlands* ('The historical task of the GDR and the future of Germany'), still spoke of the 'nation split into two states'. It introduced the process of rejecting the reunification of Germany. The GDR, it said,

cannot wait to complete the construction of socialism, to fulfil this its historical mission, until the peace-loving forces in West Germany under the leadership of the working class have achieved victory. It cannot and will not let its development be dependent on the lagging behind of the social order in West Germany, which we already lead by a whole historical epoch.

Its first programme, which the SED set itself at its VI Congress in January 1963, laid down the aims and guidelines for future economic and social policy and stated:

A new age in the history of the German people has begun: the age of socialism ... The GDR has already entered this new, socialist age in Germany ...

The descriptions of the overall world political situation and of communist future prospects in the SED party programme were borrowed from the party programme of the CPSU, which had been adopted at its XXII Congress in October 1961. The central point of this programme, however, lay in its outline of economic development.

In the economic sphere the serious weakness caused by the flight of specialist workers to the West was gradually to be made good by a new economic orientation. In 1963 the GDR, encouraged by the reform ideas of various theorists concerned with the planned economy, was the first Comecon country to introduce the 'New Economic System of Planning and Management' (NES), which provided for a thoroughgoing reform of the planning and management of the socialist economy. This NES was to improve the existing planning system by a better combination of long-term state planning and indirect steering of individual enterprises by means of monetary measures. The decision-making powers of individual nationalised enterprises (VEB) and their superior associations of nationalised enterprises (VVB) were increased, so as to offer greater incentives to individual enterprises through limited profit maximisation and even some autonomy in their use of profits, in order to raise the profitability and efficiency of the economy. The essential ingredients of the NES were to be greater flexibility of the planning and management system, transition from purely quantitative thinking to cost-benefit comparison, avoidance of misallocation of investment and stronger concentration on the needs of the domestic and international markets, but these could not be tackled because the reform of industrial prices with 'cost-based prices', which was to be implemented in three stages by 1967, was not carried out.

The granting to enterprises of limited responsibility for the use of their own profits, and the industrial policy pursued in the GDR, aimed at creating the desired economic structure, would have led to great disproportions if the economic reform model had been put fully into practice. Stronger centralisation, the planning of enterprise profits (to which the financing of individual plan tasks is closely linked), and the trimming of the right previously given to enterprises to participate in the investment decision-making of central authorities, considerably limit the stimulative role of profit in the 'system of economic levers'.

At the VII Congress of the SED in 1967, science was also given a completely new importance in the planning and management of the national economy. 'Science as a factor of production' was said to be becoming increasingly important in the age of the scientific and technical revolution. In the sphere of social policy Ulbricht linked cybernetics, information theory and social forecasting with the ideological premises of the SED and called for the formation of 'the socialist community of man' in which there would no longer be any class differences. In order to translate the long-term goal — the building of communism in the GDR — into somewhat more concrete terms, Ulbricht described socialism for the first time in September 1967 as a 'relatively independent social formation'. This development found its political reflection in the new GDR constitution of 1968. After the building of the wall and the start of the comprehensive construction of socialism, it became necessary to devise a new constitution for the new social reality. This new GDR constitution, the second, abolished the first constitution of 1949 and came into force on 6 April 1968.

In the sphere of social and cultural policy a new trend was observed in February 1965 in the promulgation of the 'law on the uniform socialist education system'. The second school law of 1959, which had closely followed the Soviet school reform of 1958, had already introduced compulsory ten-year general schooling in the GDR. University entrance is gained by optional and selective attendance at the two-year extended secondary school. The 1965 law did not introduce any changes of principle in the school structure. The workers' and peasants' faculties were abolished, special schools and special classes were officially introduced, and the ten-year school was sub-divided into lower, middle and upper stages, producing a fully integrated overall educational system.

On 20 December 1965 the GDR family code was passed, in which Clause 3 says of the education of children:

It is the foremost task of parents to bring up their children in confident cooperation with state and social institutions to be healthy and lively, proficient and generally educated human beings and active builders of socialism.

In this way the family was drawn fully into the socialist legal system.

A further important turning-point in the history of the GDR was the replacement of Walter Ulbricht as party chief by Erich Honecker on 3 May 1971, immediately before the VIII Congress of the SED in June 1971. Ulbricht's description of the GDR as 'a developed social system of socialism' was replaced by Honecker with the term 'a developed socialist society'. In contrast to Ulbricht, Honecker emphasised the working class as 'the crucial determining force in the development of all sectors of socialist society'. The working class now appears as the 'chief factor of production'. The party's task is 'to direct the social development of the German Democratic Republic politically on the basis of scientifically grounded strategy and tactics'. Consequently, the thesis of socialism as a relatively independent social formation with no direct relation to final conceptions of communism also had to be rejected:

This thesis obscures the fact that socialism is the first, lower stage of the communist social formation. Further, it obscures the fact — proved historically by the example of the Soviet Union — that the developed socialist society gradually grows into the communist society on the basis of the development of socialist production relations and their material-technical base.

In place of the abstract and colourful pseudo-scientific formulae which were prevalent under Ulbricht, Honecker introduced a sober assessment of the situation. In line with this went a certain mistrust of technocratic thinking, behind which lay the fear that in the GDR science could become a leading power in itself rather than merely an instrument of the leadership, in so far as its representatives gain entry into the leading party bodies in order to formulate the political and ideological objectives previously set by the SED. The SED ideologue Kurt Hager explained this very clearly:

Important as cybernetics and systems theory are and remain, we naturally cannot allow them to take the place of dialectical and historical material-ism, the political economy of socialism, scientific communism or even socialist management science, nor allow them to become unqualified, nor let the language of a specialised branch of science become the political language of the party. If that happened, the party would cease to be a Marxist-Leninist party.[19]

The increase in the ideological element under Honecker became clear in the field of domestic policy: from 1971 workers' and peasants' children were consciously given preference at the expense of children of the intelligentsia in admission to extended secondary school and university. The final elimination of semi-state enterprises and their complete transfer to state ownership, as well as the stepping up of the movement to bring handicraftsmen together into producers' cooperatives, reinforced this trend from 1972 onwards. This increase in emphasis on the ideological element is also necessary for the SED to be able to demarcate itself more sharply from the other German state with the same language, the same cultural tradition and the same history.

In foreign policy, the *de facto* recognition of the GDR by the Federal Chancellor, Brandt, in his declaration of 1969, the Treaty of Moscow of 12 August 1970, the Four-Power Berlin Agreement of 3 September 1971, the two 1970 meetings between Brandt and Stoph, at Erfurt in March and at Kassel in May, and finally the conclusion of the traffic agreement between the Federal Republic and the GDR on 26 May 1972 and the conclusion of the basic treaty between the two German states on 21 December 1972, brought the GDR its breakthrough to worldwide recognition — up to the time of writing 120 states have recognised the GDR — and admission, simultaneously with the Federal Republic, to the United Nations. This increase in meetings and contacts between Germans in the two German states at the same time leads the SED to consider a policy of sharper ideological differentiation essential.

The constitutional change of 7 October 1974, on the occasion of the twenty-fifth anniversary of the GDR's foundation, adapted the constitution to the changes in the political situation in the GDR since 1968 and established new emphases in German policy and in the state. The deletion of the concept of the German nation from the preamble is in line with SED German policy, according to which not only two German states but two German nations exist, and it binds the GDR more strongly to the USSR. At the same time the process, introduced in 1972, of taking powers away from the State Council in favour of the Council of Ministers, and now the National Assembly, is being continued.

A year later, on 7 October 1975, the GDR concluded its third basic treaty with the USSR (the first treaty was in 1955 and the second in 1964), by which it binds itself in 'eternal and unswerving friendship' to the USSR. The 'further drawing together of the socialist nations', which is found in this treaty for the first time in any international legal document, will be sought by the USSR through the conclusion of bilateral treaties with the other East European countries, in which the new friendship treaty with the GDR could serve as an example.

The strengthening of the GDR — above all, of its economic and social foundations — and its integration into the socialist community of countries, as well as its closer linking with the USSR, were carried on a further stage by the IX Congress of the SED, held on 18-22 May 1976. There Honecker continued the policy he had introduced in 1971, concentrating on the chief tasks in economic and social policy.

The new party documents adopted at the IX Congress — the second programme (the first programme was adopted in 1963) and the fifth statute (the first statute was adopted in 1946, the second in 1950, the third in 1954 and the fourth in 1963) — take account of the changes in the domestic and foreign political situation of the country. They commit the second German state to the further construction of the 'developed socialist society' as a form of 'dictatorship of the proletariat', in order to complete in this way the gradual transition to communism. The construction of a socialist society of achievement is taking place under the direction of the SED, which is emphasising its claim to leadership in all spheres (state, economy, society, science, culture, sport, etc.) even more strongly than before. In this the SED is making use of the state as its principal instrument, the executive and supervisory functions of which, far from diminishing, are reinforced on the way to stateless communism.

Parallel to the 'developed socialist society', which, according to the new SED programme, can only be created in close community with the other East European countries under the leadership of the Soviet Union, which is already building communism, there is said to be taking shape in the GDR a separate socialist nation, the nature of which is determined by the socio-economic order in existence there. German nationality, which the 'socialist nation of the GDR' will still have in common with the 'bourgeois' German nation of the Federal Republic, is said to be of secondary importance and not sufficient to form a common German nation with West Germany.

Through its signature of the Final Act of the Conference on Security and Cooperation in Europe on 1 August 1975 in Helsinki, and the preparation and holding of the conference of European communist and workers' parties on 29-30 June 1976 in East Berlin, the GDR gained in international status. The unabridged publication of the final documents of both conferences had the result that, for the first time in the GDR, a group of civil lawyers openly called for the fulfilment of the Helsinki Final Act and based themselves on the democratic socialism model of the large West European communist parties. The SED leadership, taken by surprise by this development, reacted with repression and administrative sanctions. The changes in the top state posts on 26 October 1976 — General Secretary Honecker became chairman of the State Council, Willi Stoph Prime Minister and Horst Sindermann President of the National Assembly — served to strengthen the executive. The appointment of Stoph, a well-proven organiser who enjoys the confidence of Moscow, as Prime Minister is intended to guarantee better and more effective coordination of the activity of the various specialised economic ministries as well as the more efficient functioning of the security organs.

3
State and Party Structure

Party structure

The GDR describes itself in Article 1 of its 7 October 1974 Constitution as 'the political organisation of the working people in town and country under the leadership of the working class and its Marxist-Leninist party'. Therefore in the first section we shall examine the party structure, and then outline the structure of the state.

As we have already mentioned, five parties exist in the GDR: the Socialist Unity Party of Germany (SED), the Christian-Democratic Union (CDU), the Liberal-Democratic Party of Germany (LDPD), the National Democratic Party of Germany (NDPD) and the Democratic Peasant Party of Germany (DBD). In addition, the following four mass organisations were founded in the GDR: the Free German Union of Trade Unions (FBGB), the Democratic Women's Union of Germany (DFD), the Free German Youth (FDJ) and the Cultural Union of the GDR (KB). All these parties and mass organisations are combined together in the antifascist-democratic block of the National Front of the GDR, whose political line is determined by the SED.

The NDPD has 85,000 members, the CDU 115,000, the LDPD 75,000, and the DBD 92,000. The largest mass organisation is the FDGB with 8.4 million members, followed by the FDJ with 2.16 million, the DFD with 1.3 million and the Cultural Union with 208,170. In view of its 1,914,382 full members and 129,315 candidate members (1976), the SED possesses a dual character as a party of cadres and a mass party. With 12 per cent of the total population — every sixth voter in the GDR is an SED member — party membership in the GDR is at about twice the level of that of the CPSU in relation to the total population of the Soviet Union. 56.1% of SED members are workers, 5.2% are cooperative farm peasants, 20.0% belong to the intelligentsia and 18.7% are white-collar employees and others. It should be noted that in these figures those party members who were formerly workers but have for years been professional functionaries are counted as workers. These statistics do not show separate figures for white-collar employees who are not members of the intelligentsia, students, self-employed, housewives and pensioners. The proportion of women in the SED membership amounts to 31.3%. The perceptible aging

35

of the party in recent years has been slowed down. Today some 20.1% of party members are less than thirty and 43.4% are less than forty years of age. According to data for 1976, 27.4% of all SED members have had higher or specialised education. At the functionary level, 31% of members of basic organisations, 51% of members of SED district organisations and 70% of members of county organisations have completed higher or specialised education. All of the principal professional functionaries in the county organisations are said to have done so.[20]

The SED legitimises its existence through Marxist-Leninist ideology. It claims to have a monopoly of understanding of the path of development of GDR society to socialism and communism ordained by historical laws, and derives from this its monopoly of political leadership.

An applicant wishing to join the SED as the 'conscious and organised vanguard of the German working class and the working people' and the 'leading force of socialist society' should not be older than forty and must first be a candidate for one year. According to Item 19 of the SED statutes of 22 May 1976, the would-be candidate lodges an application for admission with the appropriate basic organisation. This must be accompanied by an answered questionnaire, a *curriculum vitae* and a guarantee from two party members who have been members for at least two years and must have been acquainted with the applicant through his professional and social activity for one year. After the passage of the one-year period, the candidate lodges his application for membership of the party with the appropriate basic organisation. This application too must be accompanied by guarantees from two party members. 'They are responsible to the party for an objective, expert judgement of the professional and social activity of the candidate.'

The highest organ of the party is the party congress, which has to be held every five years. The party congress receives the reports of the central committee, the revision commission and other central organs, and passes resolutions on them; it decides the programme and statutes of the party and determines its general line and tactics.

The party congress elects the Central Committee (CC), which at present consists of 145 full members and fifty-seven candidates. The CC elected on 22 May 1976 consists of ten members aged 30-39, eighty-three aged 40-49, sixty-four aged 50-59, twenty-six aged 60-69, fifteen aged 70-79 and four who are 80 or over. In comparison with the last CC, elected in 1971, it is striking that the 50-59 age group has increased by twenty members — the most notable change in age structure — so that the average age of the 1971 CC of 51.1 years has risen to 52.9 in the 1976 CC. The breakdown of the 1976 CC by occupations is as follows: seventy-one members come from the party apparatus, fifty-six from the state apparatus, twenty are economic functionaries, another twenty are functionaries in mass organisations, sixteen work in the field of culture and science, ten are from agriculture, eight are party veterans and miscellaneous others and one belongs to the NVA. It appears that the occupational make-up of the CC remains relatively constant: 'This applies particularly to the party, economic and agricultural apparatus but also to the field of culture and science. Detailed analysis has shown that those whose main field of activity is the economy have gained greater importance. . . The same is true of agriculture. The increase in numbers from the state area is smaller; the representation of the mass organisations has risen strikingly. The increase to twenty representatives of mass organis- ations in the 1976 CC can be attributed substantially to the greater significance given to FDJ functionaries.'[21]

The CC, which must hold a plenary session at least every six months, has to carry out the resolutions of the party congress, delegate 'representatives of the party to the highest management organs of the state apparatus and the economy', and confirm the party's candidates for the National Assembly. 'The central com- mittee guides the work of the elected central state and social organs and organisations through the party groups existing in them.' This principle of delegation is extremely important in the exercise of power by the SED.

For the political direction of its work between plenary sessions, the CC elects the Politburo, which corresponds approximately to the executive of a Western mass party, and has nineteen full members and nine candidates. The Politburo represents the collect- ive directing and leading organ in the GDR; it votes and decides according to democratic principles and in practice ultimately lays down policy for all fields in the GDR. It meets, as a rule, every week.

For the 'direction of current work, chiefly supervision of the implementation of party resolutions, and for choosing party work- ers', the CC elects the Secretariat. The Secretariat, of which the General Secretary, and thus Party Chairman, is Erich Honecker, has secretaries respectively for international relations, party organs, agriculture, culture and science, trade and supply, agitation, women, the economy, propaganda (to the West) and security. The CC Secretariat, with its forty-one departments, does not represent an independent power factor but serves to prepare decisions and to supervise their subsequent execution. This CC Secretariat in prac- tice forms the central party apparatus, with a full-time staff of over 1,000. From East Berlin it directs the whole party machinery, which consists of some 50,000 full-time and about 300,000 unpaid part-time functionaries, who were elected at the last party elections from December 1975 to 4 April 1976.

The Central Party Control Commission is also appointed by the CC. According to the SED statute of 22 May 1976 it has the following tasks: 'It protects the unity and purity of the party, fights against hostile influences and against all fractional activity. It deals with members and candidates who falsify and distort the party's policy by opportunist-revisionist formulations or dogmatic attitudes. It helps to implement party principles where the Leninist norms of party life and the rights of members and candidates are infringed and the execution of resolutions is endangered. It watches over the observance of party discipline by party members and candidates, and calls to account those who have been guilty of infringement of the resolutions of the programme and statutes of the party, of party and state discipline or of party morale.' The Central Party Control Commission's resolutions have to be confirmed by the CC.

The Central Revision Commission, similarly elected by the party congress, regularly scrutinises the 'expedient organisation and progress of the work of party organs, the party apparatus and party institutions, work on the submissions, proposals, advice and criticisms from the ranks of members and candidates and from the population, the finances and the business of the party'.

The will of the party is implemented in both state and society through the practice by which top state positions are held by members of the Politburo; at intermediate and lower levels it is done through the principle of delegation, with the party delegating its members to the various state, economic management and other functions, and at all levels it is done through the 'nomenclature' principle. The 'nomenclature' principle ensures that all leading positions are occupied only by persons who have been selected by the highest SED body at the same level, and who are for the most part SED members.

The central party apparatus also includes a number of institutes. The party institutes and party schools are for the party training which individual members have to undergo in their years of apprenticeship. The leading party institutes in East Berlin include the Institute for Sociology, the Institute for Marxism-Leninism, the Institute for Opinion Research, the Central Institute for Socialist Economic Management, and the Karl Marx Party High School. Training of party members in their apprenticeship year is carried on in 644 district and enterprise party schools, twenty-six special schools and fourteen county party schools. The Karl Marx Party High School, founded in 1946, and the Institute for Sociology, established in 1951, are for training leading personnel, who can even obtain a doctorate and a higher degree there. Of the leading party personnel 60% have been to a party school for at least one year and completed the course on the principles of Marxism-Leninism, the Party Programme and the resolutions of the Party Congress and the CC plenary sessions. According to Honecker, 1.3 million SED members and 226,000 non-party members took part in courses during the party school year 1973-4.

The structural pattern at the top of the party is repeated at county, district, town and urban county level, with the county, district or town executive corresponding to the Politburo. The foundations of the party are the basic party organisations in enterprises and residential areas. Today the SED has 74,306 of these smallest party units, which correspond to the former communist cells. There are 219 district party organisations, and over thirty party organisations within major nationalised enterprises, universities and other corporate bodies. The fifteen county party secretaries play a relatively important role in the party. They have large secretariats at their disposal and are usually members of the central committee.

As a Marxist-Leninist party of cadres, the SED is built up on the principle of 'democratic centralism', adopted from the CPSU — the chief principle of leadership — which, in the text of the SED statutes, says: '(a) that all party organs are democratically elected from the bottom upwards; (b) that the elected party organs are obliged to provide regular reports on their activity to the organisations by which they were elected; (c) that all resolutions of higher party organs are binding, strict party discipline is to be exercised, and the minority and the individual submit in a disciplined manner to the decisions of the majority'. This principle contains democratic (election from the bottom upwards) and hierarchical (decisions passed down from above) theoretical components, though in practice hierarchical centralism predominates, since the candidates elected are those proposed by the next higher party body, which also supervises the election procedure.

National Assembly

The representative assemblies of the people in the GDR — National Assembly and local assemblies — are 'democratically elected organs of state power in the socialist countries, through which the working class, under the leadership of its Marxist-Leninist party and in alliance with the cooperative farmers, the intelligentsia and the other working strata, exercises political power'.[22] The political foundation of socialist democracy in the GDR is the dictatorship of the proletariat (democracy *vis-à-vis* the working class and its party, and dictatorship *vis-à-vis* the bourgeoisie as the ruling class of capitalism), and the economic foundation is the social ownership of the means of production (nationalisation of enterprises, factories, shipyards, mines, banks, etc.) which form the prerequisite for the planned economy — one of the most important instruments of the party's rule. The close connection between politics, the economy and ethics, and the identity in practice of state and society, are typical of such a socialist democracy.

According to Article 48, para. 1, of the constitution, the National Assembly is the supreme organ of state power in the GDR. It is elected by the citizens for a period of five years in 'free, universal, equal, secret ballot'. The same applies to the election of the members of county, district, city and urban county assemblies and parish councils. Five parties and four mass organisations are represented in the National Assembly and the local assemblies according to a strict formula. Every citizen of the GDR who has reached the age of eighteen years on election day is entitled to vote. Eligibility for the National Assembly and local assemblies also starts from the age of eighteen.

Under a legal regulation passed in 1965, more candidates are now put up in every constituency than there are seats to be filled, so that the GDR citizen at least has the possibility of crossing out two or three candidates from the list; a candidate must have his name crossed out by more than 50% of the electors to be rejected. Theoretically the elector has the right to cast his vote in a polling booth, yet since — so the official argument runs — no one should be prevented from voting publicly, a considerable measure of civic courage is involved in seeking a polling booth in order to vote. In doing so the elector would be sure to attract the full attention of the electoral district board. Since in any case the elector does not have the choice between opposing parties, he has no possibility of registering a negative vote other than crossing out the complete list of National Front candidates or abstaining from voting altogether. Since work brigades and housing communities are accustomed to going to vote *en bloc* early in the morning, staying away from the election demands much determination and resignation to the possibility of ruining one's career prospects.

At the National Assembly election on 17 October 1976 there was a 98.58% poll, with 0.02% spoiled ballot papers and 0.14% votes against candidates. 591 candidates stood for the 434 seats.[23] The sixty-six Berlin representatives in the National Assembly are, as in the West Berlin Chamber of Deputies, delegated to the National Assembly by the East Berlin Assembly of Deputies. East Berlin does not form a constituency, and the leading personalities in the GDR stood therefore as candidates in Karl-Marx-Stadt, Leipzig or Dresden.

To conduct the election, electoral commissions are formed in the individual constituencies, and these have a major importance because they receive nominations, decide on the acceptance of candidates and supervise their presentation in election meetings.[24] These nominations are put forward by the 'democratic parties and mass organisations', which have the 'right' — in other words, the duty — to combine their nominations with the joint nomination of the National Front.

The candidates on the National Front's combined list are presented to the electorate of the constituency at conferences of electors' representatives. If it is proposed at these meetings to remove a candidate from the list of nominations and put up a replacement candidate, the National Front has a right of veto. Such deletion of a candidate for election and replacement by another candidate only becomes legally valid when the county or republic electoral commission to which the district commission is subordinated has confirmed the decision.[25]

In view of these electoral practices, the question arises what is the sense of socialist elections at all. This can only be answered from the point of view of a completely different conception of elections, which is not based on the arbitrariness of the SED but which is derived from the principles of Marxism-Leninism. From the GDR viewpoint, the free elections in the West are not genuine free elections because they are founded on a bourgeois conception of freedom which, in accordance with its subjectivist character, allows and enables individual interests to elect parties and reject other parties. For a communist, who is convinced that the whole of mankind is developing towards communism according to historical laws, freedom consists of insight into these historical relationships. For if I know that history proceeds according to laws which are independent of man's will and influence, I no longer feel that a decision which is in accordance with historical necessities represents compulsion and lack of liberty. Hence collective voting is also understandable, since a view of history in which a deterministic development is crucial cannot accommodate any confession of individualism, nor free elections which involve the possibility of a decision against socialism.

Even though the elector in the GDR has the right to call for the removal of a deputy at the meetings of electors convened by the 'responsible committees of the National Front,[26] it does not mean that the deputy has an imperative mandate. His mandate is neither free nor imperative under the Socialist state and social order, as his continuous accountability to his electorate, which may not be reduced to a once- or twice-yearly cycle, is thought to bind him in many ways to his electors.

The deputies enjoy the right to form fractions. The 500 deputies in the National Assembly elected on 14 November 1971 formed the following fractions: SED 25.4%, CDU 10.4%, LDPD 10.4%, NDPD 10.4%, DBD 10.4%, FDGB 13.6%, FDJ 8%, DFD 7%,

and KB 4.4%.[27] Although elections took place on 17 October
1976, the above figures referring to the 1971 National Asembly are
quoted since no handbook on the deputies elected in 1976 was yet
available at the time of writing. If one looks through the biograph-
ies of the National Assembly deputies who belong to the fractions
of the mass organisations to see how many are SED members, the
SED fraction rises to 273 actual SED members or 54.6% of all
deputies, so that in fact they have an absolute majority in the
National Assembly.

By social origin, according to the official statistics, the deputies
in the National Assembly comprise 53.6% workers, 10.6% agricultural workers, members of agricultural cooperatives, individual
working farmers, gardeners and fishermen, 21.0% white-collar
employees, 5.6% members of the intelligentsia, 6.2% independent
craftsmen, 1.6% carrying on trade or business or free professions
and finally 1.4% others. The proportions, and the relationships
between fractions, are approximately the same for the local
representative bodies. 66.4% of National Assembly deputies are
men and 33.6% women. By age groups, 3.0% of the deputies are
in the 18-20 age group, 5.0% are 21-25, 4.0% are 26-30, 15.4%
are 31-40, 40.0% are 41-50, 26.0% are 51-65, and 6.6% are over 65
years old.[28]

According to the introductory article to section 3 of the GDR
constitution, on the structure and system of state direction, the
activity of the peoples' representative bodies in the GDR, as the
implementation of the principle of 'sovereignty of the working
people', is conducted on the basis of democratic centralism. This
principle, adopted from the SED, became state law by its extension
to the state sphere. It means: election of the organs of state power;
accountability of peoples' representative bodies, deputies, judges,
state and economic managers; decisions by higher state organs are
binding, and state and administrative discipline is strict.

Thus not only does the party determine the policy of the National
Front, and not only do the deputies and state functionaries belong
to the respective SED basic party organisations in the individual
ministries and are obliged to execute party resolutions and tasks,
since they were delegated to the state organs by the party, but the
whole state is constructed on the organisational principle of a class
and cadre party. Furthermore, at the same level as any state organ
there is always a corresponding party organ, which is not of course
directly empowered to give instructions but which often meets
together with the responsible government organ.

The National Assembly elects a Presidium for the period for
which it is elected, on which the direction of the National
Assembly's work devolves according to its standing orders, whereas
in the old version of article 55 the Presidium of the National

Assembly was only charged with the direction of plenary sessions of the assembly. The Presidium, of which Horst Sindermann became chairman at end of October 1976, having previously been Prime Minister, includes representatives of all the parties and mass organisations represented in the National Asembly. The National Assembly is convened by the Presidium, and also at the demand of at least one-third of the deputies. Since the most recent constitutional changes, the National Assembly can only be convened by the State Council for the first session after elections. Previously the State Council had to examine all bills submitted to the National Assembly and arrange for their discussion in the commissions of the Assembly. All basic tasks which arose from the laws and resolutions of the National Assembly between its sessions were likewise performed by the State Council. After the constitutional change of 7 October 1974, the relevant article was revised or reformulated so that these tasks formerly undertaken by the State Council pass to the National Assembly. This indicates that the Assembly's position in the GDR state system has been strengthened and its importance enhanced.

The National Assembly, as the supreme organ of state power in the GDR (Art. 48 of the Constitution), decides the fundamental questions of state policy. It 'determines the aims of the development' of the GDR 'through laws and resolutions which are absolute and binding for everyone, lays down the principal rules for the cooperation of the citizens, communities and state organs and their tasks in the execution of state plans and social development', and 'determines the principles for the activity of the State Council, the Council of Ministers, the National Defence Council, the Supreme Court and the Attorney General' (Art. 49 of the Constitution). The Chairman and members of the Council of Ministers and the State Council, the Chairman of the National Defence Council, the President and judges of the Supreme Court and the Attorney-General are chosen by the National Assembly and can be removed from office by it at any time. Under the Constitution, the National Assembly ratifies state treaties of the GDR, can arrange for the holding of plebiscites, and can decide on a state of emergency in the country, which can be declared by the State Council in cases of urgent necessity.

The right to bring forward legislative proposals is enjoyed both by the deputies of the parties and mass organisations united in the National Front, which are represented in the National Assembly, and by the Commissions of the National Assembly, the State Council, the Council of Ministers, and the Union of Free German Trade Unions.

National Assembly deputies have the right 'to address enquiries to the Council of Ministers and to each of its members' (Art. 59 of the Constitution), and 'to take part in sessions of local peoples' representative assemblies in an advisory capacity' (Art. 58 of the Constitution). Under the Constitution, the list of duties of National Assembly deputies includes holding regular office hours and discussions with their electorate. They are obliged to take note of proposals, comments and criticisms from their electors and to see that they are conscientiously settled (Art. 56 of the Constitution).

While in practice no debate of legislative proposals takes place in the few sessions of the National Assembly — the sixth Assembly, elected in 1971, met eighteen times in all[29] — this does occur in the commissions of the GDR parliament, whose importance has recently been increased. Furthermore, important laws are often discussed at length by the whole population, although this did not happen with the most recent Constitutional revision of 7 October 1974, in violation of Art. 65 para. 3 of the Constitution.

The work of the commissions proceeds in accordance with 'overall social requirements'. Their activity cannot be compared with that of Western parliamentary committees, for the deputies still have no great possibility of influencing legislative proposals. In no case can they alter the substance of a law. The sessions of the commissions are more for the purpose of enabling deputies to express their opinions. Previously the activity of the commissions was also directed by the State Council, which decided whether bills should be discussed in the commissions, though the National Assembly may have taken the initiative.[30] Article 70 acquired a completely new content in the constitutional change, so that the written restrictions on the activity of the National Assembly and its commissions no longer apply.

In so far as the National Assembly did not make arrangements itself, the agenda of the plenary sessions was also submitted by the State Council, which also prepared the sessions of the National Assembly. After the change in the constitution all these functions have passed to the National Assembly. The writs for elections to the National Assembly and to the other representative assemblies however are still issued by the State Council.

The sixth National Assembly elected passed sixty-one laws in its period of five years.[31] There can be no clearer demonstration that the National Assembly is a relatively powerless body and that its activity in the function of making laws is very modest. Its existence can only be justified in so far as its sessions decide the fundamental questions of state policy. Up till now all bills have always been unanimously adopted by the National Assembly. For the first time in the history of the GDR parliament, in the vote on the law on the termination of pregnancy on 9 March 1972, according to *Neues Deutschland*, there were fourteen votes against and eight abstentions, primarily by CDU deputies.[32]

State Council

The political structure of the GDR, as a state with a socialist world outlook, is better understood if we rid ourselves of the Western conception of the division of powers based on Montesquieu. In the GDR state power forms a unity, which is only exercised by different instruments. Thus the state is not separated from the party but rather, is the executive organ of the resolutions of party congresses, CC plenary sessions and the weekly Politbureau meetings.

As a result of the constitutional changes of 7 October 1974 the following powers were surrendered by the State Council to the National Assembly: 1. The State Council no longer represents the National Assembly between its sessions. 2. The State Council now convenes only the first session of the National Assembly after elections have been held. Thereafter convening of National Assembly sessions is the task of the National Assembly Presidium. 3. The State Council no longer has the power to deal with legislative proposals and examine whether they are in accordance with the Constitution. 4. The State Council is no longer authorised to make laws by decree. The State Council only takes decisions 'for the execution of its duties'. 5. The constitutional law-functions no longer devolve on the State Council but are handed over by it to the National Assembly.[33]

The State Council is elected by the National Asembly at its first session after elections for a period of five years. The nomination for the election of the Chairman of the State Council is submitted by the largest fraction in the National Assembly, which is always the SED (Art. 67). 'The State Council represents the GDR internationally. It ratifies and revokes state treaties and other international agreements for which ratification is prescribed' (Art. 66, para. 2). The State Council is answerable to the National Assembly for its activity. It issues the writs for elections to the National Assembly and to the other representative assemblies (Art. 66 and 72). 'By order of the National Assembly the State Council assists the local representative assemblies as organs of the unified socialist state power, promotes their democratic activity in the formation of a developed socialist society and exerts its influence for the preservation and lasting establishment of socialist legality in the activity of the local organs of the people' (Art. 70). The State Council exercises the rights of amnesty and pardon and undertakes continuous supervision of the 'constitutionality and legality of the activity of the Supreme Court and the Attorney General' (Art. 74). 'The State Council takes fundamental decisions on questions of the defence and security of the country. It organises the defence of the country with the help of the National Defence Council. The State

Council appoints the members of the National Defence Council. The National Defence Council is answerable to the National Assembly and the State Council for its activity.' (Art. 73).

After the death of Walter Ulbricht the former Prime Minister, Willy Stoph, became chairman of the State Council. The assumption of the chairmanship of the State Council by Honecker, the party chief, at the end of October 1976 makes constitutional what was already political practice, namely that the GDR is represented on important occasions for foreign policy by the General Secretary of the SED. Honecker thus combines in his own person the top posts in party and state (party chief, Chairman of the State Council, Chairman of the National Defence Council) like his predecessor Ulbricht. Yet it must not be overlooked that Honecker is chairman of a State Council whose powers he himself reduced, but whose political importance within the framework of its responsibilities could nevertheless increase. Besides the Chairman there are twenty-four other members of the State Council. The Chairman and the Secretary are full-time posts. The numerical composition of the State Council is not laid down in the Constitution, which only speaks of the Chairman, his deputies, the members and the Secretary. The Chairman has seven deputies, who belong to the SED, the CDU, the LDPD, the NDPD and the DBD. One member of the State Council is a non-party member, the Chairman of the National Council of the National Front, Professor Erich Correns. Of the total of twenty-five members of the State Council, sixteen belong to the SED, two to the CDU, two to the LDPD, two to the NDPD, and two to the DBD.

The National Defence Council, which is responsible and accountable both to the National Assembly and the State Council, is the 'leading state organ in the GDR for the unified direction of the defence of the country'. It was established in 1960. The National Defence Council in practice functions as an auxiliary organ of the State Council for the organisation of the defence of the country. Fundamental decisions on questions of defence are taken by the State Council itself. The National Defence Council consists of at least twelve other members beside the Chairman. The Chairman is elected by the National Assembly, and the other members of the National Defence Council by the State Council. The importance of the National Defence Council is underlined by the fact that the Chairman is the party chief, Erich Honecker, and the Secretary is Lieutenant-General Fritz Streletz. It is not known who the other members are, but it can be assumed that they include the top party and state functionaries responsible for defence, security and emergency planning.

The Council of Ministers

The Council of Ministers, which is elected by the National Assembly and the chairman of which is provided by the strongest fraction in the National Assembly, that is to say the SED, is not a complete government in our Western sense but rather an executive organ for the decisions of party congresses. With its forty-two members it would not work effectively as a Western-type cabinet either. For this reason a smaller circle, the Presidium of the Council of Ministers, was formed, with sixteen members. The Chairman of the Council of Ministers, Willi Stoph, has two first deputy Chairmen, Werner Krolikowski and Alfred Neumann, and nine deputy chairmen. Besides the traditional departments, with Army General Heinz Hoffmann as Minister for National Defence, a number of specialist ministers, who are in practice the directors of various branches of the economy, belong to the Council of Ministers. Thus, for example, it includes a minister for machine tools and processing equipment, for the glass and ceramics industry, for construction, a minister for county-controlled industry and the food industry, for agriculture, forestry and foodstuffs, for coal and electricity, a minister for ore mining, metallurgy and potash, for the electrical and electronic industries, and so on. Basically the Council of Ministers is a large economic board which manages 'the GDR Ltd.'.

Recently the Council of Ministers has often met jointly with the Central Committee. In order to strengthen the Council of Ministers for its function of managing the economy — some three quarters of its decisions relate to economic management — the Council was given various State Secretariats and Offices like, for example, the State Planning Commission, the Office for Atomic Safety and Protection from Radiation, the Office for Youth Affairs, the Supreme Construction Authority, etc.

The law of 16 October 1972 on the Council of Ministers of the GDR and the constitutional change of 7 October 1974 strengthened the position of the Council of Ministers *vis-à-vis* the State Council. They ended the original division of work whereby the State Council should deal with fundamental problems of the leadership of the state and the Council of Ministers with the detailed preparation of essential basic decisions for the National Assembly and with the direct management and organisation of the execution of the laws and resolutions of the National Assembly and the implementation of the principles laid down for it by the State Council. The Council of Ministers has now become the central organ for economic, planning, and government administration, the duties of which grow as higher demands are made on administration, planning and the economy.

The Workers' and Peasants' Inspectorate, the chairman of which is Albert Stief, has the task of 'organising the systematic supervision of the practical execution of the resolutions and directives of the party of the working class, of the laws and resolutions of the National Assembly of the GDR, of the decisions of the State Council of the GDR and of the decrees and decisions of the Council of Ministers, with the help of a comprehensive people's control system, contributing to the improvement of management and planning and consolidating state discipline and socialist legality'. The Chairman of the Committee of the Workers' and Peasants' Inspectorate is a member of the Council of Ministers and holds the rank of Minister. Subordinated to him there are county, district and town committees of the Workers' and Peasants' Inspectorate, as well as elected branch- and group-inspectorates. These institutions exist in enterprises in industry, transport, construction, trade, foreign trade, in nationalised farms and agricultural cooperatives. People's Control committees and groups operate in towns, residential areas and parishes.

The members of the Workers' and Peasants' Inspectorates and the People's Control Committees, which are also subordinate to the basic organisations of the SED, are elected for a period of two years at enterprise and residents' meetings. The members of the workers' and peasants' inspectorates are unpaid and cooperate closely with the trade unions' workers' supervisors, the FDJ control points, the National Front Committees and other social and state organs with supervisory functions. The workers' and peasants' inspectorates, which have extensive rights, conduct their activity primarily in an educational manner, employing the press, radio and television to broadcast their information and criticism. The corresponding body to the executive organ of the Council of Ministers at county level is the county council, at district level the district council, at town level the town or urban county council and at parish level the parish council. The principle of dual subordination generally applies to all the various councils: as councils elected by the local representative assemblies as local executive organs they are horizontally accountable to their respective assemblies. As organs of local state power they are vertically subordinated to their superior council. In practice the horizontal subordination is more of an appendage in comparison to the substantially more relevant vertical subordination, which, where conflict occurs, prevails over the horizontal subordination. When necessary, the superior council invokes its equivalent representative assembly which among other things has the right to participate in sessions of its subordinate assemblies in an advisory capacity, so as to be able to use its influence against an undesirable decision. Furthermore, it should not be forgotten that, as in the National Assembly, the SED forms the largest fraction in the local representative assemblies.

Since the deputies are delegated to the assemblies by the party, they are subject to party resolutions and must carry out party tasks, so that in this way possible real conflicts between vertical and horizontal subordination can be prevented through the party.

Legal system

In the ideology of Marxism-Leninism law belongs to the super-structure which spans the socio-economic base. All changes in the conditions of ownership of the means of production in this base are reflected in changes and upheavals in the superstructure. Every social formation thus possesses its own legal conceptions. Conse-quently the law is in this sense class law, for, as a component of the superstructure, it has the function of legitimising and protecting the existing conditions of ownership in the base. Since in the socialist state of the GDR the means of production have passed into the ownership of the people, the majority of whom consist of the working class, the law in the GDR is an expression of the rule of the working class and its vanguard, the party. From this point of view the administration of justice has to be done on a party basis. In this sense the law, or 'socialist legality', serves as an instrument for consciously changing and moulding GDR society. 'Socialist law incorporates the objective regularities of socialist society and thus works as a lever for their conscious implementation'.[33] The function of law which is customary in the Western democracies — a means to ensure internal order — is also exercised by the law in the GDR, but the other function of the law described above is superimposed on it.

A typical example of the attitude of a socialist society to the law is provided by a passage in the 1963 decree on the administration of justice, which declares, on the principles of socialist justice, that 'socialist law is an important instrument of our state for the organisation of social development'. The law or the legislature in the GDR thus does not have the function of limiting and restraining the executive power of the state but, on the contrary, since it is not an independent third force, it is an instrument in the hands of the party and the government for implementing policy, of which the basic features are decided at the SED party congresses, in accord-ance with circumstances and the historical laws which are believed to lead inevitably to an eventual worldwide communist society. The objectivity of the law, of laws, of the administration of justice, etc. in the socialist society of the GDR thus consists not in the avoidance and absence of political and social influences but, on the contrary, in the fact that the law, both in the form of the laws and in the administration of justice, is in harmony with the 'objective regularities of social development' which, driven by the motor of the class struggle, ultimately leads to the victory of the working class and its party. The socialist law of the GDR does not recognise the natural law which derives from the nature of man and is a basis for state law. 'Socialist legality' demands that the positive law laid down by the state be formulated and applied according to party principles. Yet the party basis of the administration of justice must guarantee the legal security postulated in Article 19 of the GDR constitution.

The GDR constitution recognises and guarantees basic rights of the citizen, which are however different from our Western conceptions of basic rights. Whilst the basic rights in our Western states are seen in general as individual rights to freedom, which the state has to respect, the basic rights in the GDR are not rights of the citizen *vis-à-vis* the state, guaranteeing him a private sphere free from the state and protecting him against state encroachments, but they serve to guarantee the individual participation in the life of the state and to integrate him into the political process. Since in a socialist society the contradiction between individual and collective interest is increasingly eliminated, it is not necessary for these fundamental rights to create for the individual an area of freedom from the grip of the state, for the individual's own interests are in full harmony with the political and ideological interests of society as a whole and its ruling instrument, the state. Thus it is understandable that the GDR constitution should give central importance to the 'right of co-determination and joint moulding of society' (Articles 19 and 21).

In Articles 19 to 40 the following basic rights are enumerated: personal freedoms — freedom of the person, postal and telephone secrecy, freedom of movement within the area of the GDR state, inviolability of dwelling, freedom of conscience and faith and the right to profess one's faith and participate in ritual actions; political rights — freedom of expression of opinion, of the press, radio and television, freedom of assembly and of association; rights of participation — exercise of the general right of co-determination and joining in the moulding of society through elections, participation in state and social life, accountability of state and economic organs, expression of will by means of the parties and mass organisations, petitions and plebiscites; fundamental social rights — the right to work, the right to education and participation in cultural life, the right to leisure time and a holiday, the right to protection of health and capacity for work, the right to social welfare, the right to housing; institutional guarantees — guarantees of the institutions of marriage, the family and motherhood, the right of parents to bring up their children, the guarantee of personal property, the right of inheritance, copyright and the right of patent (Art. 11); rights to personal protection — claim to legal protection when outside the GDR, ban on extradition. The current extent of the personal freedoms is to be inferred from the relevant legal regulations, the political rights are subject to a constitutional reservation, the implementation of the fundamental social rights is only possible within the limits of social requirements and economic conditions and the institutional guarantees only apply within limits drawn 'in the interests of society'. The principle of equality (Art. 20) runs through the whole list of basic rights. It is expressly forbidden to discriminate in respect of nationality, race, world outlook and religious creed, social origin and position; men and women have equal rights.

The guarantees which assure the basic rights in the GDR are not so much juridical as political (i.e. the existing distinctive political system), economic (i.e. state ownership of the means of production and central planning and management of the economy) and ideological (i.e. obligatory Marxism-Leninism).[34] That this is not sufficient is shown by the civil rights initiatives seeking nothing more than the full implementation of the basic rights guaranteed in the constitution.

A characteristic of the understanding of basic rights in the GDR is the close connection between rights and duties, such that in many cases the rights are to be interpreted as duties. According to the arguments of legal theorists in the GDR both form an indivisible unity. The rights are to be understood as obligations to exercise them actively. This is most clearly expressed in Article 23, the first paragraph of which says: 'The protection of peace and the socialist fatherland and its achievements is the right and the honourable duty of the citizens of the German Democratic Republic. Every citizen is obliged to serve and contribute to the defence of the German Democratic Republic according to the laws'.

Under Article 92 of the Constitution the administration of justice in the GDR is exercised by the Supreme Court, the county courts, district courts and social courts within the framework of the tasks given to them by the law. In military cases the Supreme Court, the military higher courts and military courts exercise jurisdiction.

The Supreme Court, which is elected by and is responsible to the National Assembly and, between sessions of the Assembly, to the State Council, is the highest organ of the administration of justice in the GDR.

'The Supreme Court directs the administration of justice by the courts on the basis of the constitution, the laws and other legal regulations of the German Democratic Republic. It ensures the uniform application of the law by all courts' (Art. 93 of the Constitution). The Supreme Court discharges this function of direction by formulating guidelines and by the decisions of its presidium. Between 1953 and 1971 a total of twenty-nine such guidelines were issued.

Besides the Supreme Court there are fifteen county courts and
altogether 249 district courts.[35] These courts employ 1200 professional judges and almost 50,000 lay assessors. The judges, assessors
and the members of the social courts — 'only a person who is
loyally devoted to the people and the socialist state can be a
judge...' (Art. 94) — are elected by the representative assemblies
(judges, lay assessors and the arbitration commissions of residential
areas) or directly by citizens (conflict commissions by the workforce, and arbitration commissions in production cooperatives by
their members). They have to deliver reports to their electors and
can be dismissed by the latter if they 'offend against the Constitution or the laws or otherwise fail seriously in their duties' (Art. 95
of the Constitution).

A new institution in the GDR legal system is the creation of
social courts, which operate either on application by the injured
party or on the basis of a decision by the police, the state attorney
or state courts to transfer a case to them. The social courts —
conflict commissions in enterprises and arbitration commisssions in
residential areas and in production cooperatives — handle labour
law cases and civil law cases where the value of the object of dispute
does not exceed 500 Marks, as well as offences, omissions and
irregularities of any kind remitted by the state attorney[36] in the
first instance, which may not be circumvented. These social courts
reduce the load on the state courts and have the effect of
diminishing the number of criminals, for they are not intended to
punish the guilty but to educate them. At present 37% of those
answerable to criminal charges are handed over to the social courts.
In addition an annual average of 15,000 civil law disputes are
settled by the social courts. The social courts thus take a major
burden off the state courts, which can therefore concentrate on
more serious kinds of criminal offences.

According to Article 95 the judges, lay assessors and members of
social courts are independent in their administration of justice and
are bound only by the Constitution, the laws and other legal
regulations of the GDR, though the fact that judges are not
appointed for life but elected only for the period of a legislature —
and have no great degree of security — does not help to ensure this.
Lay assessors, who, according to Article 96, exercise the 'function
of a judge in full measure and with an equal vote with professional
judges', lack legal training. Instead they are sent to take special law
courses and training programmes. These lay judges are proposed
by the parties and mass organisations and coordinated in the joint
lists of the National Front. This procedure for recruitment of lay
judges guarantees to a substantial extent the party basis of the
administration of justice in the GDR.

In criminal law in the GDR the educative function of punishment is emphasised more heavily than the sanction. On the other hand, however, for political crimes the punishment has the nature of a deterrent because of its severity. In contrast to the criminal law of the Federal Republic of Germany, in the GDR, for political crimes, not only committing the crime but the attempt or preparation to commit a political crime are subject to severe penalty. Offences of this kind are betrayal of peace, enlistment in imperialist armed forces, war-mongering, fascist propaganda, gathering information, supporting imperialist organisations, treason against the state, conspiring to cause damage, attacks on means of communication, illegal crossing of the frontier and excessive rowdyness, which would be equated with offences involving demonstrations. In the GDR there is no longer a distinction between imprisonment and penal servitude and the highest punishment is the death penalty.

As a rule in the GDR there are two levels of proceedings for appeal against the verdict of the first instance at district or county level or at the supreme court. The legal institution of revision does not exist in the GDR. Instead, the county courts and the Supreme Court have the possibility of quashing verdicts of the first instance.

In accordance with its understanding of law the GDR has no constitutional court. The task of examining the constitutionality of legislative proposals therefore falls upon the National Assembly. Similarly the GDR has no administrative jurisdiction. The attorney general of the GDR is Josef Streit (SED) and the president of the Supreme Court is Heinrich Toeplitz (CDU).

The frequently repeated view that the crime rate in the GDR is substantially lower than in the Federal Republic of Germany must be examined rather more closely. From the available figures we can state generally that where the crime rate among young people is concerned a rising trend is clearly observable in both German states. First offenders' readiness to commit a crime can be seen as similar in both states. But the statistics on crimes are not immediately comparable primarily because, after the introduction of the new criminal procedure in the GDR in 1968, crimes have been recorded in a different manner to the Federal Republic and, furthermore, the operation of the social courts as conflict commissions in enterprises and arbitration commissions in residential areas has permitted an extensive reduction in the number of crimes of theft. (N.B. In 1975 225,623 members took part in 25,358 conflict commissions in enterprises and administrative bodies and 53,448 people participated in 5,127 arbitration commissions in residential areas and production cooperatives). In terms of crimes per 100,000 inhabitants, the Federal Republic's rate is eleven times higher than the GDR for fraud, about ten times higher for robbery and blackmail, and five times higher for arson, murder and manslaughter. In the GDR half of all crimes are committed by young people under twenty-five years old. According to the most recent statistics published by the GDR, in 1969 800 fourteen to sixteen year-old and 1900 sixteen to eighteen year-old criminals per 100,000 of the same age were caught (the figure for the Federal Republic in 1974 was 3,953 fourteen to sixteen year-olds).[37]

4
The Economy

The system

As we described in the chapter on history, all the enterprises in the GDR were gradually transferred to national — i.e. state — ownership. The final step in this direction was taken in 1972, mainly for ideological reasons. In agriculture, collectivisation of private farm land led to the formation of agricultural production cooperatives (LPG) and nationalised estates (VEG). While the agricultural land brought into LPGs remains the private property of the farmers, the land and other means of production in VEGs are state property. There are three types of LPG in the GDR: in type I the land is collectivised, in type II the land, machinery, tools and traction power for crop production are collectivised, and in type III all agricultural means of production, except for those used on the individual household plots, are collectivised. In all three types the farmers can work a plot of 0.5 hectare in their leisure time for their own consumption, and also keep two cows, two sows with their young, five sheep and as many small livestock as they wish, and they may sell the produce themselves. For more than ten years there has been cooperation on a contractual basis between the LPGs, VEGs and GPGs (market gardening cooperatives) on the one hand and the food industry and trade network on the other through the formation of cooperation institutions. Such associations link vertically enterprises involved in the production of a certain agricultural product, and also enterprises which process the products and distribute them through the trade network. In 1975 there were 306 LPGs of types I and II with 10,806 members and 4,260 type III LPGs with 809,714 members. In 1975 there were 463 VEGs. In 1975, 8.0% of the agricultural land of the GDR was worked by the VEGs, 86.6% by the 4,566 LPGs, 0.4% by the 287 GPGs and 5.0% by other enterprises. In 1976, 10.95% of all those employed in the GDR worked in agriculture. Grain yield in 1974-76 averaged 35.8 quintals per hectare (39.8 in West Germany) and for potatoes the GDR figure was 152.7 (West Germany average 239.7).

In the skilled crafts sector craftsmen in similar trades were brought together into production cooperatives (PGH). In 1976 there were 2,792 PGH in the GDR with 143,076 members and a total revenue of 5.5 mlrd. Marks. In 1972 around one third of the PGHs decided to transform themselves into nationalised enterprises, officially because their production was now defined as industrial in character. The shares in the cooperatives were paid out to the members.[38]

As far as internal trade is concerned the following ownership forms are distinguished in trade enterprises: socialist wholesale enterprises (SGB), nationalised retail trade in trade organisations (HO), cooperative retail trade in consumer cooperatives, and other socialist trade. In addition there are still some private retail trade businesses and commission trade. The entire banking system is nationalised.

Nationalised enterprises (VEBs) are legal entities and operate according to the principle of economic accountability, which rests on the principle of 'achieving the highest possible revenue with the lowest possible expenditure', so as to ensure continuing high profitability and earn the maximum net profit. The head of a VEB is the Director, who bears personal responsibility. The workforce participates in the management of the enterprise through the SED enterprise party organisations and the FDGB enterprise trade union organisations. The VEB may be a member of a Combine — horizontal integration — or of a trust-like amalgamation of different VEBs in the same branch of industry into an Association of Nationalised Enterprises (VVB) — vertical integration, which likewise have to operate on the basis of economic accountability. The various VVBs are under the direction of the specialist ministers in the Council of Ministers, according to branch. The combine is legally an independent, nationalised enterprise, with a high level of concentration of production, integrating several stages of production previously produced independently in separate enterprises, on the basis of their technological and organisational connection. About 75% of the industrial production of the GDR is centrally controlled. The remainder, called 'county-managed industry', is under the direction of the county economic councils. The county planning commissions are responsible primarily for infrastructure projects and training of labour.

The VEBs produce on the basis of indicators in national economic plans. These may be divided according to time span into twenty to thirty year forecasts, long-term economic plans which run for fifteen years, medium-term five-year plans and short-term annual plans. National economic plans are constructed in several stages: first, on the basis of plan directives passed by the SED party congresses, the State Planning Commission works out a draft plan. The state targets based on it are then, at the second stage, communicated to all state and economic management organs, enterprises, combines, and institutions by the State Planning Commission, the Ministries and economic management organs. At the third stage, on the basis of these state targets and the results of discussion of the plan in the enterprises, in which as many of the workforce as possible are supposed to take part, draft plans are worked out by VEBs and institutions, defended to their superior organs and coordinated at all levels. The final decisions on the national economic plan and the issue of state plan targets to the state and economic management organs, enterprises, combines and institutions is then the fourth and last stage of plan construction. This socialist economic planning — the first essential element in the planned economy of the GDR — requires the socialist, i.e. state, ownership of the means of production — the second essential element — in order that it can function at all. The third essential element of the GDR's planned economy is state price-setting and the fourth is the state monopoly of foreign trade.

The reforms of the economic planning system mentioned in the chapter on history have led to certain disproportions in the economy. The conflict between individual enterprise and overall economic interests, which appears insoluble, has led in recent years to an unambiguous declaration in favour of central direction of the course of the economy. The 'decree on the tasks, rights and duties of nationalised enterprises, combines and VVBs' which came into force on 1 May 1973 concentrates the fundamental decisions in the central administration, with powers of decision on subsidiary questions delegated to subordinate state and economic organs and enterprises. This is intended to ensure the uniformity of state economic objectives without completely ignoring the multiplicity of individual economic processes and local peculiarities. In this sense the new decrees leave individual enterprises and combines a considerable measure of freedom about what measures they wish to take to fulfil the plan targets with which they are charged or what methods they use for 'self-monitoring' of their economic performance. The counter-plan movement is intended to induce workers to take on obligations exceeding plan targets. The counter-plan only conceptually appears to be in contrast to the plan, and in fact contains achievements to be attained in addition to the plan, for the purpose of organised overfulfilment. Numerous competition movements, various distinctions and bonus payments are supposed to form a substitute for competition.

Problems

The justification given by the GDR for adopting this kind of planned economy is its aim of a more just distribution of national income, better satisfaction of the material and cultural requirements of the population and smaller frictional losses than in the market economic system, as a result of the central planning of demand, production and the necessary investments, which are concentrated above all in heavy industry. In practice the GDR planners have more concern for economic growth, full employment and rising productivity and neglect the profitability of their 'GDR

Ltd'. This problem of the planned economy is thoroughly familiar
to the planners in the GDR and they have to struggle daily to
combat it. The obsolete 'cult of the gross' (planning in quantitative
rather than qualitative magnitudes), the distortions in the price
structure of raw materials like coal, gas, electric power, wood,
iron, brick and building stone — the prices of which the state
subsidises by up to 60% — lead to wasteful use of them. Furthermore, overcentralisation of decision-making saps the interest,
initiative and satisfaction derived from responsibility at the lower
levels of management.

The GDR seeks to prove, and in some areas has successfully
proved, that a modern industrial society can be built and managed
not only by market economy methods but also without private
capital and independent entrepreneurs, without a convertible currency and the market and price mechanism of supply and demand,
by methods of economic planning. The price of this mode of
functioning of the GDR economy — it does function, even if it
does not produce the abundance of commodities typical in the
West — is that its cost levels are relatively higher than in the West.
Its approximately equal economic growth costs the GDR more
capital than the Federal Republic, and this has to be provided by
limiting the quantity of supplies to the private consumption sector.
During 1960-1970 the Federal Republic used its capital 33% more
efficiently than the GDR.

Despite the notable rise in the standard of living in the GDR in
comparison with its earlier low level, the lag behind the Federal
Republic, in spite of approximately equal growth and productivity
advances, has, in fact, not diminished, but increased drastically. In
1960 the GDR worker achieved 76% of the West German real
income level, in 1969 61% and in 1972 only 55%. Even if the faster
growth of incomes in West Germany can be attributed to an
incomes explosion — real income in the GDR grew faster than in
the Federal Republic in 1973, as in 1963 and 1967/68 — the
question of the profitability of the GDR economy remains.[39]

A further obstacle to efficiency has proved to be the lack of
incentive to innovate and the failure to innovate quickly. Here it
should be remembered that, because of its 'technology gaps'
vis-à-vis the Federal Republic, the GDR cannot install the most
modern technology in its enterprises.

In 1975 the GDR produced a gross social product per head of
population of $3,200, far behind the Federal Republic ($6,830), yet
ahead of Italy, Ireland and Spain (gross social product per head in
1975 in US dollars was 8,320 in Switzerland, 8,210 in Sweden,
7,020 in Denmark, 7,020 in the USA, 6,630 in Canada, 6,280 in
France, 5,970 in the Netherlands, 5,050 in Austria, 4,370 in Japan
and 4,050 in Great Britain). The annual average rate of growth of

the gross social product from 1960 to 1972 amounted to 3.4% for the GDR and 3.7% for the Federal Republic of Germany (Switzerland 2.9%, Sweden 3.2%, Denmark 3.8%, the USA 3.0%, France 4.7%, the Netherlands 4.1%, Austria 4.3%, Japan 9.4%, Great Britain 2.3%, Italy 4.4%, Ireland 3.5%, and Spain 5.8%).[40]

Present situation

The fulfilment of the national economic plan for 1977 gives the following picture: national income produced grew by 5.2% (plan: 5.5%). Industry made a good contribution to this with a growth rate of 5.4% (plan: 5.1%) but agriculture, because of the drought and consequent harvest failure, fell behind its planned figure. The major difficulties with which the GDR economy has to struggle include the increased cost of raw material imports from the Soviet Union, its indebtedness to the West and the generally more complicated economic situation. During 1976 investments had increased by 6.8%, and in 1977 the rise amounted to 6.0% (plan: 6.5%). The net money incomes of the population rose by 5.4% and retail trade turn-over by 4.3%. In accordance with the social policy decisions of 27 May 1976 the minimum monthly gross wage was increased from 350 to 400 Mark and monthly gross wages of up to 500 Mark were subject to differential increases. Exactly 106,826 newly built dwellings were handed over for occupation in 1977.

The five-year plan for 1976-80, which was approved by the Central Committee and the National Assembly in December 1976, sets out the following lines of development for the GDR economy: owing to the difficulties we have enumerated above, economic growth is to be even slower than anticipated in the May 1976 directives (27.9% instead of 27-30%). In order to be able to pay for the dearer raw material imports increased efforts must be made to export, but only a small part of these are to be at the expense of private consumption. Consumer prices are to remain stable, but a slightly smaller growth of private consumption (net money incomes of the population and retail trade turnover) is envisaged. In order to achieve the still considerable rates of growth an appreciable increase in labour productivity (by 130% in industry) is required, which is primarily to be achieved through an economical approach to raw materials, full utilisation of available machinery and faster introduction of the results of scientific research. To promote scientific and technical progress, the 'principle factor in intensification', 35 mlrd. Marks are to be spent in the coming five years, 14.5% of the total investment allocation. Altogether investment is to grow almost twice as fast during this plan period as during the previous five years. The highest growth rates are to be seen in the sectors of industry which are important for exports — engineering, electrical and electronics, and chemicals.[41]

According to the data in the 1977 statistical yearbook of the GDR the supply of high-value consumer goods to the population has increased, as a result of great efforts by the state, but is still far from satisfactory; for example, the waiting time for a car, after paying the price in advance, is still five years or more; yet in the number of cars per 100,000 inhabitants the GDR is at the top of the list of Comecon countries. (A 26 h.p. Trabant car costs 8,000 Marks, a 1-litre 45-50 h.p. Wartburg costs 17,750 Marks and the West German Volkswagen 'Golf' costs 19,000 Marks). The supply of basic foodstuffs today is long since assured, and indeed consumption per head of fat, bread and cereals in the GDR is the highest in the world, very much to the distress of health policy experts and nutrition scientists in the GDR.

The average monthly gross income of all GDR households reached 1,766 Marks in 1974, of which 326 Marks were accounted for in deductions. The monthly gross wage for industrial workers in 1974 amounted to 846 Marks. While foodstuffs and services are as always cheap in the GDR — in 1978 they were subsidised to the extent of 14.2 mlrd. Marks (10.9% of the State budget) — relatively high prices must be paid for high quality consumer goods. The party leadership admitted to shortages of knitwear, mens suits, girls clothes, shoes, stockings, furniture, suitcases, coffee pots, cups, plates and washing powders. According to present plans, in 1980 all households should have a refrigerator, 80% of households a washing machine and 97% a television set. Great efforts are to be made to achieve an urgently needed improvement in the sphere of services of all kinds.

As far as housing is concerned the GDR clearly lags behind the Federal Republic of Germany. Whereas the size of the average dwelling in the Federal Republic in 1974 was 86.8 square metres it was only 58.0 square metres in the GDR in the same year. The GDR's difficulties with housing consist not so much in the shortage of houses, although it is greater than in West Germany, but that the houses are relatively old and often in a bad state of repair, and many are inadequately equipped. 38% of the housing stock of the GDR was built before 1900 and 41% between 1900 and 1945. In contrast, 52% of the houses in the Federal Republic were constructed after the war, as against only 21% in the GDR. The number of dwellings per 1000 inhabitants was almost the same in 1974 (376 in the GDR, 374 in the Federal Republic). According to the report by the General Secretary, Honecker, at the IX SED congress in May 1976, a total of 750,000 houses are to be created by new building and modernisation between 1976 and 1980, of which 550,000 are to be newly built. If this ambitious housing programme is fulfilled some 2.2 million inhabitants of the GDR would receive better housing. In 1975 a four-person household in the GDR spent 4.4% of its net income on rent, electricity, gas, water and heating, a corresponding household in West Germany 20.8%

The comparatively bad housing situation in the GDR can be attributed to the conditions of house ownership and distribution. Unless still privately owned, the respective commune is the owner of houses and dwellings. Whilst in West Germany the rent is often four or more times as great as in the GDR, in the latter both the commune and private landlords can only ask a lower, state-fixed rent which can in no way suffice to cover the cost of maintenance of the buildings and renovation work. The consequence of this is that housing owned by communes deteriorates and private landlords, since they cannot maintain their houses out of the low state-fixed rents, would like to sell them to the commune, which does not buy them from them. Private landlords cannot let their houses themselves, for the housing office controls all housing and allocates it centrally, since it is scarce.

The foreign trade of the GDR reached a total volume of 85.5 mlrd. foreign trade Marks in 1976, of which imports were 45.9 mlrd. and exports 39.5 mlrd. This was a nominal total increase over 1975 of 11.1 mlrd. foreign trade Marks which after allowing for price increases amounted to a real rise of 3.6 mlrd. (1974-5). In money terms the rise in total turnover was 14.87%, with imports growing 16.88% and exports 12.62%. The trade deficit of the GDR to the OECD countries at the end of 1975 amounted to $3.7 mlrd. (compared with the USSR $9.8 mlrd., Poland $6.7 mlrd., Hungary and Romania $2.3 mlrd. each, Bulgaria $2.0 mlrd., Czechoslovakia $1.0 mlrd.). The relatively high nominal growth rates were the result of price increases, which amounted to 11% on imports and 7% on exports (in 1975). By regions, 63.93% of the GDR's foreign trade in 1976 was with the Comecon countries (including Albania but excluding Yugoslavia) (-2.3% compared with 1975), 28.33% with the Western industrialised countries (+2.39%), 4.59% with the developing countries (+0.22%) and 3.16% with the socialist countries not belonging to Comecon (China, N. Korea, Vietnam and Yugoslavia) (-0.30%). With the individual Comecon countries the picture was as follows: USSR 32.51% of total GDR trade (-3,16%), Czechoslovakia 8.80% (-0.49%), Poland 8.75% (-0.15%), Hungary 5.97% (+0.55%), Romania 3.56% (+0.85%), Bulgaria 3.24% (+0.03%), Cuba 0.94% (+0.12%), Mongolia 0.08% (-0.02%), and Albania 0.07% (-0.04%).[42]

From the USSR the GDR obtains 90% of its oil, iron ore, wood and cotton, 70% of its zinc and 60% of its aluminium. This is also a major source of machinery and equipment. Thus for example some 30% of the tractors employed in GDR agriculture come from the USSR. On the other hand, the GDR provides about one quarter of Soviet requirements of machinery and equipment.[43]

The USSR is not in a position to meet the GDR's rapidly rising demand for oil (which increased by 9.8% in 1975) with additional deliveries, so the GDR will have to obtain about 10% of its oil requirements from the non-Communist market. In addition, the USSR doubled the price of oil with effect from 1975, though it still charges up to 40% less than the world market price. Whereas, hitherto in Comecon, bilateral fixed price contracts were concluded for five-year periods, the USSR has now insisted on an annual price revision clause. The fixed price is based on an average world market price from which short-term fluctuations are eliminated.

Since the USSR is no longer prepared to bear the high costs of the extraction and transport of raw materials alone, a general agreement was signed at the XXVIII session of Comecon in June 1974 in Sofia by the USSR, Poland, the GDR, Czechoslovakia, Hungary, Romania and Bulgaria on cooperation in developing a natural gas field and building a 2750 km. gas pipeline from Orenburg in the Urals to the Western border of the USSR. Under the agreement the USSR develops the gas field whilst the other Comecon countries each build a section of the pipeline. The GDR is responsible for the construction of a 550 km. stretch through the Ukraine from Kremenchug to Bar. The pipeline is to be finished in 1978 and will supply 15.5 mlrd. cubic metres of natural gas a year to the Comecon countries.[44] The extent of GDR participation in raw material projects in the USSR will certainly quadruple in the period from 1976 to 1980 and reach the order of 7-8 mlrd. Marks. In addition the GDR has not only concluded supplementary trade agreements for 1976-1980 with all the Comecon countries but also bilateral protocols on the coordination of economic plans.

Besides their trade relations, 'socialist economic integration' is proceeding in Comecon, in answer to the further integration of the EEC. The GDR chairs three out of twenty one Permanent Commissions. These are commissions for sectors which are crucial for growth or modernisation, like chemicals, construction and standardisation. The East German economic leaders offered Comecon cooperation only in areas where they could derive advantages from this cooperation. Thus the GDR had a decisive influence on the Comecon plan for a 'system of electronic accounting techniques'. In the field of computer production and in container transport the GDR exploited its competitive advantages and took a dominant part in working out a container transport system which was obligatory for the whole of Comecon.[45] Within Comecon the GDR achieved the highest standard of living because it has the highest level of industrialisation. Unlike the other East European countries, perhaps with the exception of Czechoslovakia, the GDR was able to build on a broad industrial experience and a well-trained skilled labour force. In respect of money income per head and money holdings the GDR heads the list of all Comecon countries; in respect of numbers of durable consumer goods per head and housing space it shares the leading position with Czechoslovakia, closely followed by Hungary.

Among Western countries the Federal Republic of Germany is still as always the most important trading partner of the GDR. Intra-German trade accounted for 6.4% of East German trade in 1976. In 1977 intra-German trade increased by 3.1% overall compared with the previous year, with West German purchases rising by 3.4% and deliveries to the GDR by 2.8%. The GDR's deficit on this trade rose in 1977 by 390 m. accounting units (1 accounting unit in intra-German trade has the value of 1DM or 1 Mark). In order not to let the accumulated balance rise still further the GDR paid 2.97 mlrd. accounting units in payment for deliveries from West Germany in 1977. The Federal Republic's deliveries to the GDR consist primarily of machinery and electrical products, textiles and crude oil. The GDR supplies firstly textiles, followed by agricultural products, oil products (produced from the crude oil supplied by the Federal Republic), chemical products, machinery, electrical products and iron and steel. Intra-German trade, with a total volume of 8.67 mlrd. accounting units in 1977 [46] accounts for approximately 1.7% of West German foreign trade turnover.

Intra-German trade makes the GDR an EEC country for foreign trade and it enjoys the corresponding customs advantages. The 'swing', or interest-free overdraft facility, under the new regulation of 6 December 1974, must not exceed a ceiling of 850 m. accounting units/DM per year. Whilst the Federal German government persists with intra-German trade primarily for political reasons — it is the only area in which the GDR recognizes and practices special relations between the two German states — for the GDR it is highly attractive from the economic point of view (freedom from tariffs, rapid delivery of modern technology and good service, interest-free credit).

5
Education and Training

Aims

The 'uniform socialist education system' which was introduced in the GDR in 1965, according to Article 25 of the Constitution, aims to educate a 'socialist personality'. The *Dictionary of Socialist Youth Policy* published by the SED publishing house Dietz in 1975 defines the 'socialist personality' as a 'fully developed personality, knowledgeable on political, specialist and general scientific matters, with a firm class standpoint and a Marxist-Leninist view of the world, distinguished by high mental, physical and moral qualities, imbued with collective thought and behaviour and participating actively, consciously and creatively in the development of socialism'.

The educational aim of the 'socialist personality' postulates (1) an education which is not neutral in terms of the view of the world it teaches, but (*a*) a Marxist-Leninist education of pupils and young people which (*b*) trains them in socialist behaviour. The class character of this education is determined by the intention to fulfil the historical mission of the ruling working class, to abolish capitalist society and to construct socialism and communism and spread them throughout the world.

The verdict of the Catholic bishops on the aims of the education system, contained in a pastoral letter read at all Catholic services in the GDR on 17 November 1974, was as follows: 'A complete education is however considerably endangered when the state demands a monopoly of education. This not only limits parents' and children's choice of form of school, kind of education and profession, but bases education on a one-sided view of man. The exclusive foundation of all education plans and curricula — from nursery school to university — is the dialectical materialist view of the world. The whole of life is to be stamped by this ideology. Neutrality of world outlook is rejected. Accordingly only socialist morality is presented as correct, which includes education in hatred.'

(2) Patriotic education strives to educate young people in the 'love of the German Democratic Republic and pride in the attainments of socialism, in order to be ready to bring all the forces of society to bear to strengthen and defend the socialist state'. Young people are to be educated in the 'spirit of peace and friendship between peoples, socialist patriotism and internationalism' (Clause 5 of the 'Law on the uniform socialist education system of the German

Democratic Republic' of 25 February 1965). Thus young people have not only to defend their state, the GDR, but also its particular political character and, in addition, under the name of 'socialist internationalism', the territory and social order of the other East European countries.

(3) 'Socialist education' takes place through the collective, as a medium of education, and for the collective, as an educational aim. The collective is not to be confused with the community or the team. The most important feature distinguishing it from the community is the inner connecting link between the individual members of the collective with their various social roles: their common socialist ideas. Members of the collective are imbued with these ideas or are to become convinced of them through the collective education process.

(4) Young people are to be educated, according to the education law, in the 'love of work, and respect for work and the working people'. Thus again work is both a medium and an aim of education. Education for work is to lead to a situation where work is no longer seen merely as a means of obtaining the commodities necessary for living but becomes a 'matter of honour'. The creative character of the work performed in the collective is to become more and more prominent, so that work becomes a need.

Methods

The 'uniform socialist education system' comprises the following coordinated stages: crêches and nursery schools, pre-school educational institutions, ten-year general polytechnical secondary schools (POS), extended secondary schools (EOS), special schools, specialised schools, professional training institutions, educational institutions leading to higher education, engineering and technicians' schools, universities and higher educational institutions, institutions for further education of adults.

Socialist education in the GDR has to begin in the parental home. Section 3 of the 'family law book of the German Democratic Republic' of 20 December 1965, on the upbringing of children, states: 'It is the foremost task of parents 'to bring up their children in confident cooperation with state and social institutions as healthy, lively, able and well-educated people and active builders of socialism'. This upbringing is continued in nursery schools and since 1968 has to be based on curricula for nursery schools and pre-schools and covers both education in the native language and social education of children. Since in the GDR 82.6% (1975) of all women of working age are in employment, good conditions exist for exercising influence on children at an early age. In 1975 75.5%

of all three to six year olds attended nursery schools. From the age of five onwards children begin pre-school education, which is either done at nursery schools or at 'learning afternoons' which take place every second week and last around ninety minutes.

The ten-year general polytechnical secondary school (POS), which was introduced in 1959 under the second school reform in the GDR, is intended to give all pupils a broad, well-based general education with a practical orientation. About 10-12% of pupils leave school after the eighth year.

Marxism-Leninism pervades all subjects, and most clearly in history. According to historical materialism the history of mankind proceeds within various social orders, beginning with primitive society, through slave-owning society, feudalism, capitalism, with imperialism its decadent ultimate form, to socialism and communism. Social and economic relations are decisive for this development according to historically predetermined laws in the dissolution of the old and the revolutionary formation of the new social order. Religion is attributed to the inability of early man to explain natural events rationally owing to his ignorance. The churches, and above all the mediaeval church, are alleged to be nothing but instruments of domination to console and suppress the exploited masses in the interests of the then ruling class.

The subject 'Citizenship', previously called 'Contemporary Studies', is consciously intended to influence the political views and world outlook of pupils. Here the knowledge acquired in the individual subject courses is synthesised and generalised and applied to the support of Marxism-Leninism. The aim of this is to develop scientifically grounded convictions about the world in the pupils and to teach a socialist attitude.

The polytechnical instruction, from which the schools take their name and the general character of which has been increasingly emphasised in the last two years, is allotted a total of 4.5 hours per week from the seventh year (higher stage) onwards. It builds on the basis of workshop and school-garden instruction which is given one to three hours per week in classes 1-6. The polytechnical instruction encompasses the subjects 'Introduction to socialist production' (with two courses, 'industry' and 'agriculture'), 'technical drawing', and 'productive work by pupils in socialist enterprises', which is done at the work bench in sponsor enterprises and on neighbouring agricultural production cooperatives. The polytechnical instruction is intended to impart a general technical and economic education in the principles of production processes and capacity, and readiness for productive work.[47]

The entire school system is centrally controlled by the Ministry of People's Education in East Berlin. Outline and detailed curricula for each subject and each class lay down the object of the course, so that the teacher does not have much scope to decide what is taught. In addition, under the 1967 decree on schools, a plan of work for the school, class plans and a plan for out-of-school education have to be drawn up. As there are no cultural authorities at subordinate levels, instruction is based on centrally published textbooks, which are pedagogically well constructed. In every lesson there is an oral test of the preceding lesson in the subject. At the end of each school year performance in a written examination in the major subjects determines advancement to the next class. The examination papers are sent out to the teachers by the Ministry of People's Education in a sealed envelope, so that they are unknown to the teachers themselves until the start of the examination.

Mathematics and the natural sciences are pursued particularly intensively in schools in the GDR, at the expense of arts subjects. Russian is a compulsory subject from the fifth class. A second foreign language can be taken optionally from the seventh class by pupils whose performance in the first foreign language is good. In the two year extended secondary school a second foreign language is a compulsory subject. Overall the whole scheme of education in the GDR is directed towards performance. Competitions in various subjects at school, city, county and republic level are intended to search out outstandingly gifted pupils. These pupils (0.05% of all pupils) are then collected in specialised schools on the Soviet model, in which the special subject is taught more intensively, at the expense of other subjects. In the GDR there are specialised schools and classes for sport, music and dancing, acrobatics, foreign languages, mathematics, physics and technical subjects.[48]

Out-of-school education is undertaken by the Young Pioneers (736,000 members in 1975) for six to ten year olds, the Thälmann Pioneers (1.13 million members in 1975) for eleven to fourteen year olds and the Free German Youth (2.16 million members in 1975) for young people over fourteen. Almost all school children are involved in the pioneer organisation, and it should be noted that the pioneer groups are disbanded in the eighth class in order to prepare the young people for entry into the FDJ. The work of the youth organisations takes in on the one hand the usual forms of youth activities (establishment of 107 'pioneer houses', 212 'young technicians and mature students stations' and 43 'young tourist stations'), and on the other supports the teaching and education of the schools and higher educational institutions. Helping with the harvest, taking part in demonstrations arranged by the state, collection of waste paper, non-ferrous scrap metal, old bottles and bones and also money, for example for the Vietnam Solidarity Fund, are the order of the day. Pioneer uniform, badges of rank, parades in the school courtyard at the beginning and end of each week, flags of pioneer friendship of each school, pioneer emblems (drums and trumpets) in the pioneer room at every school, a professional pioneer leader in every school with a seat and voice at the staff meeting, election of group council chairmen for each class and friendship council chairmen for each school, preparation of political 'wall newspapers', badges for good knowledge, participation during the holidays in pioneer camps with a military regime — all this gives the pioneer activities a strong political, propagandist and quasi-military accent.

Overtly ideological instruction, with preparatory courses for the youth dedication ceremony in which up to 90% of all school children take part, courses of instruction in preparation for entry to the FDJ, and the weekly FDJ hour in school, and the establishment of 'young socialists' circles', is entrusted to the only youth organisation in the GDR, the FDJ. In the FDJ school year which started in November 1976 there were 65,000 people engaged in teaching these courses. The FDJ, with 98,318 basic organisations, is represented in every school and higher education institution, every factory and LPG, and every barracks. The sociological breakdown of its membership gives the following picture: at least 80% of all students, secondary school pupils, apprentices, officers and national servicemen in the National People's Army (NVA) are members as are about 50% of young workers who have completed their training, about 40% of unskilled young workers and 20% of young LPG farmers and workers on nationalised estates. [49] The relatively weaker representation of young people in full-time employment in the FDJ is explained by the fact that they tend to join the FDGB instead. A second reason may be that they are less concerned about career advancement. The FDJ, which, as a mass organisation, belongs to the National Front, has the right to send deputies to the National Assembly and county assemblies and to form a fraction there. In the present National Assembly in East Berlin the FDJ accounts for 8% of the deputies. 32.6% of the representatives in the GDR parliament (the 1971 National Assembly) are aged between twenty-one and forty. The same thing applies to the representation of the FDJ in district councils, city assemblies and parish councils.

The FDJ participates directly in the management and supervision of the state administration and the economy. The GDR labour law book prescribes, for example, that in all questions which affect young people in enterprises the enterprise management has to cooperate closely with the organs of the FDJ. According to Clause 137 of the 'labour law book of the German Democratic Republic' published on 12 April 1961 the FDJ has the 'right to organise supervisory units in order to contribute to the development of high socialist morale and new methods of work and to the introduction of the latest techniques and to lead the struggle against defective work. The enterprise director has to support the FDJ leaders in the direction of the FDJ supervisory units and regularly to instruct the supervisory units in cooperation with the FDJ leadership. He is obliged to carry out suitable proposals put forward by the FDJ supervisory units.'

In addition young people in the GDR are increasingly being drawn in for economic tasks. For this purpose youth brigades are formed, in which a 'collective of young people' carry out certain parts of the work process over a longer period. There is a general attempt in the GDR to give young people responsibility early. Relatively young people occupy leading positions much earlier than in the Federal German Republic. Their 'householder function' is pointed out again and again to young people in the GDR, that is to say, that they will soon be master in their own state. By entrusting 'youth projects' to young people, the party and the FDJ accustom them to responsibility early. Their ambition is aroused in that they are offered the opportunity to achieve something; and, at the same time, the inevitable grumbling dissatisfaction of young people is skilfully contained. The FDJ annual review for 1973 shows that in that year 21,252 youth brigades were in operation and 59,051 youth projects were carried out. The largest FDJ youth project yet is the 'FDJ Initiative Berlin', launched in September 1976, with the help of which 200,000-230,000 new houses are to be built and 100,000 existing ones modernised in East Berlin by 1995. The FDJ campaign 'Save Materials Year' (1973) produced a benefit of 338 m. Marks in 1973; 75,000 tons of scrap were collected. At the annual 'Central Fair of Craftsmen of Tomorrow', in which 1.7 million young people took part in 1973, around 1500 scientific and technical achievements were displayed, the aim of two thirds of which was to increase labour productivity, reduce costs and save labour time.

Youth advancement plans, which are drawn up every year, serve as 'the leading instrument for enterprise managers' for political and general philosophical education, the treatment of general questions of social policy and problems of science and technology and the communication of general technical and cultural values. Under the provisions of the labour law an enterprise manager has to report on the fulfilment of the youth advancement plan to the enterprise trade union leadership (BGL), the FDJ leadership and the young people at the enterprise.

The third GDR youth law, of 1 February 1974, fills out, in its fifty-nine paragraphs, the details of Article 20 of the GDR Constitution: 'Young people are particularly encouraged in their social and professional development. They have every opportunity to play a responsible part in the development of the socialist social order'. This youth law, which was discussed over a period of six months by 5.4 million citizens of the GDR at 240,000 meetings, and into which — according to official sources — 4800 proposals for changes were incorporated, differs from both its predecessors in the following points: it is more specific about its measures, for instance in naming those responsible for implementing them; it strengthens the position of the FDJ leadership; it stresses the role of the working class and the SED more strongly; it underlines the increased orientation towards the USSR and other socialist countries; it makes a consistent demarcation *vis-à-vis* the West and refers more definitely to the GDR as the socialist fatherland; it adopts in the text for the first time the clause on the honourable duty of defending socialism.

Together with the Society for Sport and Technical Affairs (GST), with Major-General Teller as its chairman, the FDJ carries out the pre-military training of young people in the schools. The members of this organisation, to which 95% of all male and female young people over the age of fourteen belong, can choose the discipline of all-round military competition, shooting, motor sport, 'signals sport', air and sea sports, diving and 'model sport'. According to the new programme of the central council of the GST dating from 1 September 1973 training of young people in shooting is to be intensified. As well as higher demands in physical training, education in defence and politics is to be strengthened by dealing with themes such as 'The military superiority of socialism', 'The sense of being a soldier', 'No chance for the enemy', and 'Youth — the army of socialism'. The formation of circles called 'Young friends of the People's Army' and the holding of military competitions and manoevre games are intended to help to bring up children as socialist patriots.

Parents' representatives in the GDR have a legally established right to consultation on school problems, starting for example with school meals and including questions of teaching methods and careers advice, but not on the construction of timetables and the establishment of curricula. For this purpose parents' advisory councils were formed for every school in 1951 and parents' groups, consisting of between three and seven members, for each class in 1967. The parents' advisory councils of the 5875 schools in the GDR, with five to twenty-five members, are elected for a period of two years. They meet regularly (at least once every two months) and have an annual plan of work. Those parents who 'actively support the work of the school in socialist education and upbringing' are eligible for election. The parents' advisory council always includes a representative of the school's patron enterprise and of the DFD, a delegate from the education workers trade union and a representative of the relevant committee of the National Front. In 1974/75 the 103,961 members of the advisory councils and 572,951 members of the parents' groups were newly elected. This means statistically that one parent in every fourth family in the GDR with a child of school age is a member of a parents' group or advisory council.

The 'patron' enterprise — an industrial or trade enterprise chosen by each school as a patron and bound by a patronage agreement — is supposed to support the teachers by making enterprise installations available, and by cooperation from its experts. The polytechnical training of the pupils is to be carried out jointly by the teachers and suitably qualified employees of the enterprise in the school and in the patron enterprise. In addition the enterprises are expected to set up specialist departments, equip classrooms and help with the maintenance of the buildings and the vacation training of the pupils of the schools of which they are patron. The para-military 'enterprise fighting groups' are responsible to the FDJ and SED basic organisations for effective pre-military training in the school of which the enterprise is patron. This is done in close cooperation with the NVA, which sends soldiers to the schools for friendship meetings, invites pioneers to open days at barracks and makes them acquainted with military equipment.

For children and young people who are seriously handicapped, physically or mentally, but are capable of school education, there are special schools. These schools, which take handicapped children (who are subject to registration) from one or more districts or counties, are generally boarding schools.

As far as choice of profession is concerned, careers advice based on the 'principles for the further development of professional education as a component of the uniform socialist educational system' (11 June 1968) is intended to ensure that the personal wishes and interests of young people are thoroughly coordinated with the requirements of the national economy. Permission for training is issued by the district council, observing the prescribed quotas for training for the various occupations. Professional education in the GDR was completely reorganised in 1967. The new decree on training, which applies compulsorily throughout the GDR, introduced twenty-eight basic professions and forty-nine broadly defined training specialisations into which all those previously existing were combined. After leaving secondary school (POS) the apprentice learns one of the basic professions in the first year and then, in the second year of the two-year course, is trained in one of about 700 specialised professions. Today in the GDR almost 60% of all professional schools are specialised enterprise schools which from 1957 onwards have been combined with the enterprise apprentices' workshops and apprentices' hostels to form 'uniformly organised training establishments of socialist enterprises under the charge of the works directors'. The ratio of time spent on theory to practice in training is 2:1, though in the second year practical training is predominant. An introduction to electrical

technology and data processing is a compulsory part of all professional courses. A small proportion of apprentices receives the
opportunity to take their *Abitur* (approximately the English General
Certificate of Education) in the *'Abitur* classes of professional
educational institutions' in a training course which is extended by
one extra year.

Direct preparation for university and higher educational institutions is provided by the two-year extended secondary school (EOS).
Pupils accepted in the EOS have completed the preparatory ninth
and tenth classes in the POS.

Like the demand for apprentices, the demand for academically
trained specialists is based on the requirements of the planned
economy. Accordingly, the number of places is increased or
reduced each year by the ministry of higher and specialised
education. In 1975 there were 136,854 registered students, which
was a decline of 5.4% compared with 1974 and of 15% compared
with 1972 (the last year when student numbers were increased).
31,000 new students matriculated at the beginning of the 1976/7
academic year in the universities and higher educational institutions.
Whereas in past years the demand for places was always substantially greater than the number available, this year for the first time
2000 fewer places were taken up than planned in 1975. In accordance
with the requirements of the economy the breakdown of places for
the 1976/7 year was as follows: 34.2% of admissions for technical
disciplines, 25.0% for secondary and professional school teachers,
11.7% for economics subjects, 7.7% for mathematics and natural
sciences, 7.1% for medicine, 5.3% for agricultural sciences and
9.0% for some twenty other specialisations. Altogether in the GDR
there are thirty-five basic courses of study with 161 disciplines.

Before admission to the last year of the extended secondary
school the pupil must submit three preferences for professions,
which are sent with the testimonials on his school performance and
social assessment to the central office in Magdeburg, where they
are collated by a computer and compared with the guidelines from
the ministry in East Berlin. If one of the three preferences can be
met 'in agreement with national economic requirements', the pupil
is invited for interview by the higher educational institution to
which he is allocated, which enables the pupil to meet his future
professors and find out more about his intended course of study
and the professors to examine the potential student to see if he
would measure up to the requirements of the course. These
interviews are more difficult when all three of the courses of study
chosen by the pupil are oversubscribed. In this case, if the pupil is
considered suitable on the basis of his school qualifications, social
and political activity and social origin, they will attempt to
persuade him to take a course in a different subject. Since

admission to higher education is regarded as a social distinction and opens up the way to professional and social advancement the pupil is ill-advised to be too obstinate in such an interview. Before the 1976/7 academic year around 5500 students, or 17.7%, had to be interviewed by teachers and lecturers at higher educational institutions in order to redirect them from their chosen but over-subscribed course to another line of study. The demand to study medicine, for example, is greater than the number of places. On the other hand there are insufficient applicants in teacher training for mathematics and physics and polytechnical subjects, enterprise organisation, automation technology, technical cybernetics, electrical technology, textile technology and certain other specialised technical subjects.

Besides school performance, according to the new admission decree of 1 July 1971, active participation in the development of socialist society, an exemplary readiness to meet all the requirements of socialist society and active defence of socialism are decisive factors in admission to extended secondary school and university. In addition, since Erich Honecker took over the party leadership, more consideration has been given to the social origin of pupils. Whilst in the mid-1960s the admission criteria had been changed towards greater emphasis on performance, not least as a result of the economic reform begun then, there is now to be an attempt to raise the proportion of workers' and peasants' children in higher education to equal the corresponding percentage of the population. Between 1960 and 1967 the proportion of workers' and peasants' children among students had declined from 50% to 38%, so that half of all students came from intelligentsia families, which accounted for only 10% of the working population. Although many children of intelligentsia members have grandparents who were workers or peasants, the minister of higher and specialised education, Böhme, made clear in 1973 that this is not sufficient reason to let the children of intelligentsia families of proletarian origin automatically grow into the 'new class'. Furthermore, those students who came to university after an apprenticeship, a period of work or service in the army proved to be particularly well motivated in their studies. The increasingly frequent cases in recent years where students have been excluded from higher educational institutions or university because of religious practice should not be overlooked.

The third higher education reform, introduced in 1966, led to a tightening up and division of higher education into several phases, greater political and ideological penetration and an even closer connection between higher education and the economy. Today every course begins with the basic studies during which instruction in the necessary scientific research methods is given, the Marxist-

Leninist view of the world is taught and the study of the Russian language is continued. Students of all faculties must pass examinations in Marxism-Leninism and Russian. This two-year basic course is followed by another two years of specialised study, at the end of which is a vocationally-oriented examination. If the graduate intends to take up an academic career he must take a further one-year specialised or research course. This thus prevents too early specialisation in a narrow field and at the same time is intended to promote comprehensive learning, in that students are involved in research projects. Research in higher educational institutions in the GDR is in large part contract research and is perhaps excessively concentrated on practical application to the neglect of fundamental research, quite the opposite to the USSR.

The GDR is aiming to make allowance for the rapid obsolescence of knowledge by shortening the first, formal education stage of learning and study and compensating for this by extending the second, further education stage. Therefore, every graduate of a higher educational institution has to take a refresher course within a period of five years.

The students at the fifty-four higher educational institutions in the GDR, including the seven universities of Berlin, Dresden, Greifswald, Halle, Jena, Leipzig and Rostock, in 1976 numbered 77.7 per 10,000 of population, compared with 134.5 in the Federal Republic of Germany in the 1976/7 winter semester. It is striking that the proportion of female full-time students in the GDR, at 53.7%, was 23.5% higher than in the Federal Republic. As well as the 101,555 full-time students in 1976 there were 19,725 external and 231 evening students. The Federal Republic has no equivalent to this extensive system of external and evening study.

Under the third higher education reform the remnants of the old professorial university were abolished in the GDR and new organisational structures introduced: the head of the university, appointed by the minister of higher and specialised education, is the rector, who is assisted by various directors, for example for training and upbringing, further education, research, planning and economy, personnel and qualifications, and international relations. The university council includes delegates from all members of the university or higher educational institution. The rector is required to render a report to it at least once a year. The faculties were finally dissolved in 1967/8. The various university institutes were combined into departments which are coordinated by leading departments in individual areas of specialisation. The scientific council, which awards academic degrees in place of the former academic senate, is constituted through elections in the departments. It also lays down research plans, and ensures cooperation between the different scientific disciplines and maintains their connection with production. The social councils, which are composed of members of the university and representatives of the economy and of local state and social organs, appointed by the minister, are supposed to take account of overall social interests in planning the work of higher educational institutions.

The students thus have, at most, a right of consultation in matters which concern their personal field. They have no opportunity to take part in drawing up the strict timetable of study — higher education in the GDR is similar to school, with compulsory attendance at all lectures and exercises checked by the FDJ — nor in the construction of curricula and the determination of syllabuses, which are all laid down by the ministry of higher and specialised education. Student representatives, who can attend various bodies, are delegated not by the student body but by the FDJ basic organisation in the university. In the bodies in which they are admitted, and in which the SED basic organisation in the university is dominant, they have 10-15% of the votes.

Students receive a basic grant, which depends on their parents' average monthly gross income and the number of children they are supporting. The maximum monthly grant of 190 Mark is given where parental monthly gross income does not exceed 1000 Mark if one parent is working. The limit is raised by 700 Marks if both parents are working. In addition, under particular conditions grants for good performance, for research, and additional and special grants can be given, so that the basic grant can be increased up to a maximum of 405 Marks. Since in 1969 65% of all students lived in a student hostel and paid 8-10 Marks per month for lodging in a two or three bedded room, and a refectory meal costs 0.60-0.80, the student on the basic grant can meet the basic living costs. Those unable to find a place in a student hostel or boarding house, or who do not wish to live in one, pay abut 30 Marks per month rent for a room.[50]

Those who have not gained admission to higher education can still, after a few years of professional training and practice, achieve entrance to university for full-time, external or evening courses through craft and engineering schools and various educational institutions for adult education. State and social adult educational institutions in the GDR include the enterprise college, village college, scientific societies like Urania and the Chamber of Technology, the industrial branch college, the Institute for Socialist Economic Leadership, the people's high school, the further education college, the television college, the parents' college, the women's college and the forms of further training through the parties and social organisations.

After the conclusion of school education and professional training of whatever kind political influence continues through the parties and mass organisations and the mass media. The forty daily newspapers published in the GDR have a total daily circulation of 7.8 million copies. The central organ of the SED, *Neues Deutschland*, published by the CC of the SED, and the SED county newspapers, reach a circulation of 5.1 million all together, or more than 65% of all daily newspapers. The seventeen daily papers of the CDU, LDPD, NDPD and DBD have a total circulation of 800,000 copies.[51] The chairmen of the State Committees for Radio and for Television are members of the CC of the SED. The daily news and comment in the mass media are provided by the agitation department of the CC of the SED.

As for the attitude of the young generation to the GDR and socialism, it must be pointed out that a critical attitude among young people in the GDR towards their state cannot be equated with rejection of socialism in general and complete uncritical approval of the social system of a Western parliamentary democracy. If young people in the GDR have come to terms with the SED, they still often refuse to support the SED actively. No German state has ever done so much for young people as the GDR. Yet asked if it has won over the young completely, it will, in its disappointment, hardly be able to answer with a unanimous 'yes'. Would the young in the GDR opt for an alternative to socialism? Certainly fewer of them than we in the West perhaps assume. Would they opt for an alternative to the bureaucratic and undemocratic socialism of the GDR? Certainly more of them than the GDR would like.

6

Social and Trade Union Policy

Social insurance system

According to Article 35 of the GDR constitution every citizen has the 'right to protection of his health and capacity to work'. This right is guaranteed under a 'comprehensive social policy', which even a socialist state needs because even under socialism there are socially weak people.

In the GDR, in contrast to the Federal Republic of Germany, there is a uniform social insurance system. As well as unemployment, sickness and pension insurance, this covers those wounded in war who are unfit for work, and former officials, and their widows and children who are unfit for work, and finally other groups not in employment like, for example, the severely injured and victims of the Nazi regime. The uniform social insurance is maintained by the FDGB social insurance scheme and the GDR state insurance scheme. Social insurance covers all methods of treatment to maintain and restore the capacity for work of a patient who was in employment. Those who are no longer in productive employment are not so comprehensively or expensively treated. Insurance is obligatory in the GDR, but the following groups are excused: spouses working without payment, casual workers and other similar people with small incomes as well as certain clergy and church employees. The predominant features of the social payments are those of a system of care, and the contributions are not related to the growing outlays as in an insurance scheme. The GDR social insurance system is financed by contributions, of which the level and method of calculation have never been changed despite the constantly rising expenditures. The consequence of this has been that for more than ten years the system has had to have subsidies from the general state budget. The uniform contribution for all benefits, with the exception of benefits on account of accidents at work or occupational illness, amounts to 20% of income for incomes up to 600 Mark per month (30% for miners), of which half is borne by the enterprises. In order to receive increased sick pay in case of prolonged unfitness for work, since 1 March 1971 those earning over 600 Mark per month must pay 10% of income between 600 and 1200 Mark per month to the revised additional pension insurance scheme, in which case the employer also has to pay a further 10%.

The services which the social insurance scheme guarantees the insured and members of their families in case of illness, accident or pregnancy, comprise free medical and dental treatment and false teeth, nursing homes and help, for which in general no financial contribution from the insured is required. In addition, child delivery in hospital and in-patient treatment are also free. Hospital care is provided in principle without time limit. Free sick care at home is limited to twenty-six weeks. Social insurance also covers treatment to maintain or improve the working capacity of the employed population and to restore their health. Sick pay is paid from the first day of unfitness for work until fitness is restored, or until a pension is established, normally for up to twenty-six weeks, with a maximum of thirty-nine weeks and up to fifty-two weeks for miners, if it can be expected that the person will recover their fitness for work within that time. The rate of sick pay is 50% of the average monthly earnings on which contributions are payable, and can thus go up to a maximum of 300 Marks per month. For a total of six weeks per calendar year it is supplemented from the pay equalisation fund of the enterprise, which makes up the difference between sick pay and up to 90% of net earnings when there are five or more children. Pay equalisation without time limit is guaranteed in cases of unfitness for work through accident, occupational illness or quarantine.

For pregnant mothers, from 27 May 1976, maternity leave of twenty-six weeks is given, twelve weeks more than in the Federal German Republic. If mothers breast feed their babies they receive a state support grant of 10 Marks per month for a maximum period of six months. In addition mothers, as members of families, also get once-for-all birth grants, financed from the state budget, of 1000 Marks, in installments, if they attend a pregnancy advisory clinic before delivery of the child, and make four visits to a mothers' advisory clinic afterwards. Further help for mothers takes the form of release of unmarried mothers from work to care for sick children for a period of two days. For this period they receive sick pay from the social insurance scheme and also enterprise pay equalisation. This entitlement is not just once per year, but each time the child is ill. If the mother has to stay away from work for longer because of the illness of the child and the need to look after it, unmarried mothers receive sick pay as support from the third day up to a total maximum of thirteen weeks per calendar year, though the pay equalisation lapses.

Under the social policy measures decided on by the CC of the SED, the executive of the FDGB and the Council of Ministers only a week after the IX Party Congress on 27 May 1976, with effect from 1 May 1977 the regulation introduced on 29 May 1972, whereby the working week for full-time working mothers with three or more children and for mothers on shift work with two children was to be forty hours, was extended to all mothers with two children. Similarly, from 1 May 1977 the working week for shift workers on a three or continuous shift system is reduced from forty-two to forty hours.

The health service in the GDR is almost completely nationalised. There are only very few doctors in private practice, since most doctors are employed in hospitals, outpatient centres and polyclinics. They draw a fixed salary and the patient is treated by the doctor on duty if he goes to the polyclinic with his ailment. Thus it can easily happen that an outpatient is treated by several doctors for the same illness. The high emigration rate among doctors to the Federal Republic before the building of the Berlin wall in 1961 seriously impaired the provision of medical care to the GDR population. As a result of intensive expansion of medical studies since then the insufficiency of the number of doctors has been to some extent overcome. In the GDR in 1976 there was one doctor per 523 inhabitants and in the Federal German Republic one per 518 inhabitants (1975). In the GDR there were 108 hospital beds per 10,000 inhabitants (excluding emergency and temporary beds), in the Federal Republic 118 (1975). In the GDR there were 4.8 dentists per 10,000 inhabitants in 1976, and in the Federal Republic 5.1.[52]

An investigation of selected notifiable illnesses, in which new cases in 1976 were counted, revealed that in the GDR per 10,000 of population 3.4 active cases of tuberculosis were notified, and in the Federal Republic 6.2 (1975); typhus and paratyphus: GDR 0.1, FRG 0.04; poliomyelitis: GDR nil, FRG 0.01; diptheria: GDR nil, FRG nil. Whilst for typhus, paratyphus, diptheria and poliomyelitis the incidence of cases per 10,000 inhabitants in 1976 was more or less equal in the two German states, it was striking that the GDR had 19.9 cases of scarlet fever compared with the Federal Republic's 5.9, per 10,000 inhabitants. For infant mortality per 100 live births the GDR, with 1.4, was ahead of the Federal Republic, with 2.3 (1974). In general it can be said that the GDR health service operates at lower cost than the West German mixed system of state and private offices and private practice, because of the low level of pay. Health care in enterprises and tuberculosis care are considerably better developed in the GDR than in the Federal German Republic.

In the field of old-age insurance there is a fundamental difference between the two German states. The GDR has no system of adapting pensions to keep up with the general trend of incomes, as is usual in the Federal Republic. The major social policy programme already mentioned raised the minimum old-age and invalid pension from 1 December 1976 from 200-240 Marks to 230-300 Marks per month. At the same date minimum pensions for accident victims and those wounded in war were raised from 240 Marks to 300 Marks per month. Pensioners (men over sixty-five, women over sixty) in the GDR are one of the groups who are the worst off economically because of their low pensions.

Social hygiene and hygiene at work are strongly promoted in the GDR. This has led to the result that the accident rate at work in the GDR is only half what it is in the Federal German Republic. Among other social payments the GDR pays a child supplement of 20 Marks monthly for the first and second children and a 50 Mark monthly state benefit for the third child, 60 Marks for the fourth, and 70 Marks for the fifth and subsequent children. The child supplement of 20 Marks per child is paid until the child is fifteen, (eighteen if it continues to attend school). The state child-benefit for the third and subsequent children, as distinct from the child supplement, is given independently of the social position and income of the parents. The social expenditure of the GDR per inhabitant amounted to 1734 Marks in 1974 (3600 DM in the Federal Republic).

Trade union organisation

The trade unions, as the 'comprehensive class organisation of the ruling working class', according to Article 44 of the constitution, 'play a major part in the formation of socialist society, in the planning and management of the national economy, the implementation of the scientific and technical revolution, the development of working and living conditions, the 'protection of health and labour, working culture and the cultural and sporting life of the working people'.

Since enterprises are the property of the people, and therefore of the majority of the people (i.e. the working class), it would be superfluous for the workers and trade unions to have the right to strike. On the contrary, the trade unions in enterprises and institutions cooperate in drawing up the plans and are represented in the social councils of associations of nationalised enterprises (VVB) and the production committees of enterprises and combines. They organise the permanent production conferences.

The chairman of the FDGB is Harry Tisch, a member of the SED Politburo. The trade unions have representatives in the National Assembly, with 13.6% of the deputies. They are also represented in the local assemblies. In the National Assembly they have the right to introduce legislative proposals. Furthermore, the trade unions in the GDR perform 'political and ideological work under the leadership of the Marxist-Leninist party and contribute to the development of socialist personalities and collective relations. The trade unions are developing increasingly as conductors of socialist competition (a principle field of trade union activity), of socialist community work, the activists and innovators movement, the permanent production conferences and other forms of mass initiative.'

If one leaves aside the political work of the FDGB — which extends far beyond what society permits trade unions in Western democracies — and its social function as manager of the social insurance of workers and employees, including special arrangements for cheap holidays, and examines only its rights to participate in operation and decision-making, the following picture is obtained: in every enterprise, beside an SED and an FDJ there is also an FDGB basic organisation, which is directed by the enterprise trade union leadership (BGL). In 1945, in the then Soviet Occupation Zone, in accordance with the decisions taken by the Allied Control Commission, enterprise councils were elected from the whole workforce. But in 1946 the FDGB began by building up enterprise trade union leaderships which could only be elected from the FDGB members in the enterprises and which were bound by the decisions of superior trade union organisations, according to the principles of democratic centralism. By means of the Bitterfeld Resolutions in 1948 the FDGB enforced the dissolution of the enterprise councils and promoted the BGL to be the sole representatives of the interests of the workforce. Since that year the BGL have in practice exercised the dual function of representing the interests both of the enterprise council and of the FDGB members in the enterprise.

The principal task of the BGL, which is re-elected every two years, is to conclude an enterprise collective agreement (BKV) with the enterprise management. This enterprise collective agreement contains agreements for the fulfilment of production plans, sets the norms and bonuses in the enterprise within the framework of the centrally prescribed plan, and includes arrangements for the purpose of improving the working and living conditions of the members of the workforce. Since the December 1970 uprising in Poland this last area of trade union activity in enterprises in all East European countries has enjoyed greater attention.

In contrast to the law on the constitution of enterprises in the Federal German Republic — labour law is not codified into a single law book in the Federal Republic — the 1961 labour law book of the GDR is confined basically to the participation rights of the workers organised in the FDGB, who are represented at enterprise level by the BGL. There is thus no question of workers sharing in decision-making in the GDR. The BGL faces the enterprise director who, in a relatively strong position owing to his powers based on the 'principle of individual management', can even set limits to the extent of participation enshrined in the labour law.

In the GDR the BGL has no influence on new recruitment to the enterprise and only a limited say on transfers. However, it does have full right of participation where formal dismissal notices and dismissals without notice are concerned. Yet frequently 'cancellation agreements' are concluded under which the BGL renounces its right of participation in formal notices and is satisfied with being informed subsequently.

The institutions of the permanent production conference and the production committee enable the workers in the GDR to exercise their right of information and recommendation concerning the economic affairs of the enterprise directly and indirectly through the BGL. (The production committee is the social organ in the nationalised enterprise (VEB) which the enterprise director has to consult 'continually on all matters affecting production', though without thereby infringing the 'principle of individual management'. The chairman of the enterprise production committee is the secretary of the enterprise SED party organisation. The BGL chairman is deputy chairman of the production committee. In smaller state enterprises the permanent production conference, which is chosen by the BGL, exercises the functions of a production committee.)

There is nothing in the GDR comparable to the Federal German Republic's law on participation in decision making which came into force on 1 July 1976. Whereas in the Federal Republic, in enterprises with a workforce of more than 2,000, employees constitute half of the members of the supervisory council, this possibility does not exist in the GDR as large enterprises do not have boards there. Even at the level of the association of nationalised enterprises (VVG) the principle of individual management by a general director applies. The social council in the VVB and the production committee in the VEB would correspond to the West German supervisory council. (Social councils exercise the functions of the production committee at the level of the VVB.) Yet, as already mentioned when describing the production committee, these bodies are dominated by the SED, which uses these organs to ensure the leading role of the party in enterprises. The SED is stronger than the FDGB and the BGL.

Whilst worker and FDGB participation at the enterprise and association level in the GDR is only possible in a limited form — the justification advanced, as for the absence of the right to strike, is that in the GDR the contradiction between capital and labour has been abolished — the FDGB has its strength in the field of participation at the aggregate economic level, which is assured both in the constitution and in the labour law book. In this sense the FDGB is very conscious of its political activity within the National Front and the people's assemblies. Likewise, the FDGB has its representatives in the state economic planning and supervisory organs.

7
Ideology and Society

The image of society in the GDR

According to its own concepts the GDR is building a 'developed' or 'mature socialist society' and in doing so is guided by the Soviet experience. The GDR holds that, so far, the USSR constitutes the only country where a developed socialist society has been achieved and is functioning successfully. This provides the state with the rationale for generalizing from the historical experience of the CPSU and using it as a framework for postulating criteria of a developed socialist society. On the other hand it is being emphasized that, in contrast to the USSR, the GDR has only recently begun with the construction of a developed socialist society, and that consequently there are certain specific features in the development of the model in the GDR. However, this by no means signifies a new version of a 'German road to socialism' as put forward by the SED in 1946 (e.g. in the article by Ackermann mentioned in the chapter on history).

In conjunction with the Party programme of the SED, which was discussed at the VI Party Congress in 1963, there was a discussion of whether it was possible to proceed directly with the building of communism in the GDR. In the end the idea was dismissed with the argument that it was necessary first of all to 'bring to full maturity [all the] advantages and motive forces of socialism'. This may have been due to the following consideration. The socialist mode of production had been introduced to all the major spheres of the economy but in 1971 almost 15% of total production was manufactured in non-socialized enterprises. In the same year there were still as many as 900,000 workers and employees in private and semi-socialized enterprises. State participation in small and medium-size private enterprises was introduced in the 1950's as a transitory stage for the complete socialization of these enterprises. Hence, in order to arrive at a complete 'victory of the socialist mode of production' it was necessary to embark on expropriation or socialization of the remaining private and semi private enterprises. This was done by Honecker after the change of power in 1972. At the IX SED Congress in May 1976, and as an extension of Honecker's measures, it was to be the main task of the Party to achieve a 'further increase in the material and cultural standard of living of the people on the basis of a high rate of growth of socialist production, improvement of efficiency, scientific-technological progress and growth of labour productivity'.

83

What are the features that characterise the developed socialist society? First, there is the desired achievement of the 'main economic task', i.e. the 'maximum satisfaction of material and spiritual needs'. This, in turn, presupposes a high rate of growth of the economy and improved supply of the population with consumer goods and services. (This does not exclude the practice that it is the state which defines what is needed.) According to the new Party programme of May 1976 economic policy is to form an 'inseparable unity' with policy towards society.

A second major task required for achieving full maturity of socialism is the 'organic connection of the scientific-technological revolution with the advantages of the socialist economic and social order'. In this sphere the SED is endeavouring to accelerate scientific-technological progress and to intensify the introduction of new discoveries to the production process at enterprise level. In this vein the new Party programme states that the 'intensification of social production' achieved in this way constitutes the 'main road' to the achievement of the 'main economic task'.

Third, the developed socialist society is characterised by a further strengthening of the leading role of the working class on the one hand, and by a narrowing of the social differences between the working class, the peasants and the intelligentsia on the other. (In essence, the emphasis on the leading role of the working class is but another way of underlining the pre-eminent position and role of the SED.)

Fourth, the mature socialist society includes full development of socialist democracy. That is to say, the role of the state in the society is to be increased and the principles of socialist democracy are to affect many more spheres of life in the GDR. In the chapter dealing with the Party and state structure in the GDR it was shown that the term 'socialist democracy' also refers to the implementation of the objectives of the working class and the Party. The withering away of the state — which is to be characteristic of a communist society — has become still more remote. Completely in contrast to this remote goal, the state under socialism (which in theory is the stage of entry for Communism) is to assert itself with all its force.

Fifth, the developed or mature socialist society is seen as possible only if there is a strengthening of the socialist consciousness of the working people. According to one of the core dogmas of historical materialism, which in turn is an important component of Marxism-Leninism, 'consciousness cannot mean anything else but conscious being, and man's being is his life in the real world'. That is to say, socialist consciousness depends on the existing social and economic conditions — the 'basis' in Marxist terminology. Socialist consciousness is consciousness of existing social relationships. Yet the development of a socialist consciousness, it is argued, does not proceed automatically in conjunction with the maturing of social conditions: it requires active involvement of the Party. The Party is to help in the formation of socialist consciousness by increased ideological indoctrination.

Finally, it is said to be another feature of a developed socialist society that the 'internationalist character of socialism' forces the countries of the 'socialist community of states' into new, qualitatively different forms of cooperation. In this connection the role of the CPSU and the USSR for the 'strengthening and development of the socialist world system' is seen as inevitably increasing.[53]

In the sphere of economics socialist internationalism finds its expression in the slogan of 'socialist economic integration'. Comecon is to be an instrument for such integration although the eastern bloc's economic organisation is based only on inter-governmental agreements which have the nature of recommend-ations but no obligatory character. Within this framework socialist economic integration is interpreted by Comecon Secretary Faddeev as being a 'process that is being shaped consciously and in a planned fashion by the communist and workers' Parties and the governments of the member countries of Comecon [and that envisages] international socialist division of labour, narrowing of differences of the national economies and creation of a modern, highly efficient structure of the national economies'.[54] As the national economies of the Comecon countries are centrally planned it follows that economic integration makes sense only if it is attempted by means of the closest possible coordination of plans and ideally by joint planning. So far there has not been any joint planning for the five-year plans; hence, efforts are being made jointly to plan and implement large-scale ventures which are of importance for the whole area of Comecon, the realisation of which exceeds the five-year planning periods.

In the official view the creation of the developed socialist society proceeds under the objective conditions of the existing socialist mode of production and is being carried out by the working class and the Party — who are the agents of historical change. In principle the citizens participate in this process but their role is not decisive. Majority opinion as manifest in elections is accepted only to the extent that it is in accordance with the 'historical laws of development', these laws in turn can allegedly only be known and correctly be put into effect by the Communist Party.

West Germany in the official image

The Federal Republic is officially being regarded in the GDR as an imperialist state. This is in accordance with the Leninist definition which considers imperialism as the highest stage of capitalism characterised by the following elements:

1. Concentration of production and capital, and the creation of monopolies which play a decisive role in the economic life of the country;
2. The merging of finance and industrial capital and the formation of a new oligarchy basing itself on finance capital;
3. Increase in export of capital;
4. Creation of international monopolies and multinational corporations which divide up the world market between themselves;
5. Conflict among the imperialist powers for redivision of the world market.

This 'classic' Leninist definition of imperialism is being applied to the existing economic and political conditions in West Germany in the following way:

State monopoly capitalism

In line with the precepts of the model of imperialism the GDR adheres to the view that the power of the monopolies in West Germany has reached a new stage due to the all-embracing economic activity of the state. ('Monopolies' in this view are big corporations which occupy such a strong position on the market that they have succeeded in maintaining their profits above average for a long time and limiting the effects of competition on profits; they do not necessarily have to be the only suppliers on the market.) Whereas formerly the state merely interfered from the outside in the national economic process, it is acting today as an economic power in its own right. In the interest of the monopolies, and in order to stabilize their dominance, the state has developed a specific system of economic levers. Instead of merely favouring the concentration process in general by means of economic stimuli and administrative regulations the state now increasingly plays the role of an active organiser and midwife for the formation of new big corporations. This, it is argued, is especially true in important spheres of the economy as, for instance, the armaments industry. 'Economic activity of the state, which previously was of a limited nature, has become comprehensive and permanent and directly influences all the spheres of capitalist economic life in the FRG [Federal Republic of Germany].'[55] Thus, expansion of the state sector of the economy, which is interpreted by some Western analysts as an indication of East-West convergence, is seen in the GDR as the very opposite, namely as a symptom of the further ripening of capitalism and as a phenomenon completely contrary to socialism.

In the opinion of East German political economists and

sociologists the inherent aggressiveness of imperialism in general, and of West German imperialism in particular, is reflected in alleged 'militarisation of the economy', the 'increasing subordination of important developments in science and technology to arms production, the high concentration of capital for armaments and its increasing importance in the economy of the FRG, as well as in the intensive efforts of the arms producers [the corporations] to secure a decisive role in important fields of military technology'. In addition to the sweeping generalisations about the nature of imperialism as being 'adventurous, dangerous and aggressive' it is also being asserted that imperialism is 'reactionary and inimical to human progress'.

At times nuances and differentiations can be found which are adopted presumably for the reason of providing GDR foreign policy with some degree of flexibility. An example of this is the distinction made by Professor Dr. Gerhard Hahn, the former Director of the Institute for International Relations in Potsdam (which is the main training institution for GDR diplomats) in *Einheit*. In his article he separates the 'most aggressive imperialist groupings', and above all the 'military-industrial complex', from those forces which 'aim at pursuing the class interests of the monopoly bourgeoisie by a policy corresponding more closely to reality and responding to the challenge of peaceful coexistence'.[56] In this connection GDR representatives at times make a distinction between imperialism as an ideological term for characterising an antagonistic social system and specific conditions in a given 'imperialist' state which may to some extent deviate from the norm.

The crisis of capitalism

Any Marxist-Leninist analysis of the monopoly-capitalist state features an examination of recurrent crises which, it is assumed, will some day lead to its final collapse. However, as the expectations or prognoses of the final breakdown of capitalism have been disappointed or proved wrong several times in the past it is now being acknowledged that 'at the end of the 1940s and at the beginning of the 1950s . . . various erroneous concepts were being spread rather widely concerning the scope and the possible rate of development of the capitalist economy'. It is also being said that 'The authors of such concepts in the final analysis ignored Lenin's explanation to the effect that imperialism is characterised by two conflicting tendencies — the tendency of progress and the tendency of stagnation — and that [even] the second tendency does not at all exclude the possibility that capitalism will grow faster than previously.' Above all, in the past two factors of crucial importance had not been taken into acount: competition between the two opposed systems and the scientific-technological revolution.[57]

In order to avoid past mistakes calls are being issued for 'concrete analysis of a concrete situation'. Such analysis would show that 'there cannot be "pure" monopoly-capitalist or state monopoly-capitalist capitalism' because in addition to the 'powerful monopolies there are also hundreds and hundreds of thousand medium, small and minute enterprises'. Also while there is a trend of concentration of capital there is also an opposing tendency, the 'process of the spreading of capital among small owners'.

Some care is being taken today not to equate automatically the 'general crisis of capitalism' with its collapse. On the contrary, it is being acknowledged that 'in some scientific and technical spheres capitalism at times is adapting itself to the scientific-technological revolution more rapidly and with greater resources than socialism. For the time being capitalism in the most highly developed imperialist states possesses a broad, differentiated, stable and in many respects more attractive supply of commodities than socialism's. It [capitalism] uses this for the manipulation of a consumer mentality in its sphere of control but also for the propagation of petty bourgeois ways of life *vis-à-vis* socialism.' The more rapid development of the productive forces under capitalism is not seen as being in contradiction to the observed symptoms of crisis but is held to be the basis for a process of decay.[58]

The 'general crisis of capitalism in all the developed capitalist countries' is expressed on the national economic level not only in the contradiction between individual material wealth on the one hand, and public or social poverty, a high rate of unemployment, inflation and 'stagflation' on the other, but also in the 'educational crisis', the 'ecological crisis', the 'misery of the cities', etc. It manifests itself on the global level in 'mutually exclusive tendencies of imperialist integration and individual national initiatives', in 'recurrent crises of currency always only barely patched up, trade wars separated by periods of armistice, and chronic crises of integration which accompany the tendency of mutual monopolist interpenetration of the capitalist economies'.[59]

The political symptoms of the 'general crisis of capitalism' are said to include mutually 'contradictory tendencies for more authoritarian and fascist methods of rule and new forms of formal, bourgeois-parliamentarian democracy' and 'more frequent Party, governmental and state crises'.

As regards characteristics of the general crisis in the sphere of culture the symptoms listed are, among others, 'modernism', 'parasitism', increase in crime, drug addiction, 'increase in the number of mentally ill persons, nihilism and being tired of life as a mass phenomenon, the emphasis on sex in human relations [and] generation conflict'.

Dying capitalism also is not immune from signs of ideological decay such as anti-communism and reformist capitalism. Whereas the former limits itself to the 'slandering' of the socialist community, the latter promotes a 'counterrevolutionary concept of evolution' and aims at the strengthening of the capitalist system. In the view of the East German theoreticians of imperialism it is therefore not surprising that 'social democratism' (the 'doctor at the sick-bed of capitalism') is entering a new period of bloom.[60] In connection with this it is interesting to note that the voluminous Soviet collective study entitled 'The Ideology of Modern Revisionism' received a new title in the East German edition by the Institute for Marxism-Leninism at the CC of the SED which reads, 'The Ideology of Socialdemocratism of the Contemporary Era'.

The reforms implemented by capitalism for the purpose of strengthening the system pose the somewhat heretical question whether they originated as a response to pressures by socialism so that in the final analysis it could be argued that it is socialism which, in the era of peaceful coexistence, contributes to the maintenance and strengthening of capitalism. Such an argument would also reflect negatively upon 'revolutionary' dynamism for spreading socialism to capitalist countries. Hence, it is being stated that 'If it is pressure exerted by real socialism, transmitted to a significant degree — objectively or already subjectively and consciously — by the class struggle of the working class, which forces imperialism to make certain concessions to the working class, this does not at all mean that one must endorse opportunist and anti-communist reform policy. Where it [such policy] shows "success" it is achieved (what dialectics of history!) primarily by the pressures of the communist world movement on imperialism.' What remains is the reproach addressed to Social Democrats that they not only want to protect 'capitalism from revolutionary upheavals' but that they also want to export 'counterrevolution to the socialist countries.'[61]

As regards the interpretation of recurrent crises or business cycles in the Western world — an important element of Marxist-Leninist political economy — economists at the Institute for International Politics and Economics of the GDR have provided analyses which are less dogmatic than the previous ideological pronouncements. In their view there have been 'significant changes' since the Second World War in the way in which business cycles run their course: the depths of cyclical recessions in production 'have lessened in most countries and cycles'; the 'cyclical downward movements often are occurring more gradually than in previous periods', and 'duration and rates of growth showed considerable differentiation from one cycle to the next both between and within individual countries'.[62]

However, these significant changes in business cycles in the opinion of GDR theoreticians do 'not at all reflect a "lessening" of the contradictions in the capitalist reproduction process or even a "stabilization" of the imperialist system'; they are rather the expression of the fundamental contradiction existing in capitalist society between the necessity of utmost 'utilization' of capital and the means which are applied to achieve it. As a consequence the 'volume of profit increases with the expansion of total capital but at the same time the rate of profit decreases with the growing organic composition of capital.' The degree to which the fundamental contradiction is being sharpened hence cannot be found in the cyclical but in the *permanent* character of capital depreciation in the capitalist economic system.[63]

Also, the 'transfer of the consequences of capital depreciation' and the 'increase in the rates of exploitation' as embarked upon by the 'monopoly bourgeoisie' are said no longer to proceed in cyclical motion but in new forms. Stagflation, 'permanent increase in the cost of living', 'increase in direct and indirect taxation on income from labour', and other similarly 'modern', 'indirect' and 'smooth methods of exploitation' are all being portrayed as symptoms of permanent crisis. The argument concludes that in the state monopolist economic systems the 'interconnections between the power of the monopolies and the power of the state' lead to a 'new interconnection between political crises and economic crises'.[64]

Anti-imperialist strategy

Reform policy, in the East German view, cannot solve the basic contradictions of capitalism because reforms 'constitute partial successes which soon turn out to be inadequate and above all unstable. Sooner or later it will be evident that one has to go further.' By means of marginal concessions the 'ruling class' of course will attempt to pre-empt the more far-reaching demands for reform, 'to change their purpose or ultimately to crush them'. As a result the demands of the 'masses' evolve 'in the direction of a principled challenge of the monopolies to battle, from the establishment of individual strongholds and positions of power to the achievement of long-term power, and from changes in the existing class relations to change in society itself'. In line with Lenin's tactical prescriptions 'one area after the other . . . is to be wrested' from the bourgeoisie in order to 'transform the half-way and hypocritical "reforms" on the basis of the existing order into strongholds for the workers' movement advancing to the full emancipation of the proletariat'. One should never forget 'that the new power does not fall out of the sky but grows and comes to life alongside and against the old power'.[65]

The road of the 'struggle for reforms', which is to be transformed at a particular stage of development into a 'form of movement for revolution', is characterized by strikes (short and sporadic strikes up to general strikes) and occupation of factories. The latter are especially important in the East German view as they already contain 'elements of violence'; violence, in turn, is seen as 'a necessary element in every serious struggle for social progress'. Although communists had 'demonstrated sufficiently' that they do 'not shrink from making necessary sacrifices' they regarded nevertheless the 'peaceful road' to socialism as the 'most desirable form of transition'. Such peaceful transition, however, will only be possible if it is feasible 'to isolate the monopoly bourgeoisie internally and externally to such a degree that it does not dare to use armed force for fear of self-destruction'. The conditions necessary for that had to be created by the 'anti-imperialist forces' by way of struggle. These are said to include a stable, militant and broad anti-imperialist alliance; maintenance and expansion of democratic rights and institutions so that it will become legal to achieve democratic progress; and strengthening of socialism, safeguarding of peaceful coexistence and cooperation with the workers' movement in other countries to such an extent that it will become impossible to import armed counterrevolution from abroad. In this connection the military potential of the socialist community of states constitutes a decisive instrument for safeguarding peace and preventing armed counterrevolution. This strategy depends on the preservation of Parliament, for inherent in parliamentary majority is the 'formal right of forming a government which can be used as an important instrument for [achieving] power'.[66]

Should power be gained by the parliamentary road it follows that this is not merely to be regarded as a victory achieved by the national working class of a given country but credit is due also to the 'struggle of the working people' of all the countries and 'international unity of action'.[67]

Within this framework special importance is attributed to the 'working class'. Lenin identified the working class with the industrial proletariat because under the then existing conditions the industrial proletariat was seen as the only class that 'could develop a revolutionary class consciousness under the leadership of the Marxist party of action'. But in contemporary conditions the question arises whether the imperialist state in the era of the scientific-technological revolution has not created the 'objective preconditions for the inclusion of additional social groups' to the working class. This is a question that can by no means be answered in the GDR in a way similar to that suggested by Western Marxist ('revisionist') theoreticians such as Marcuse or Garaudy. Instead the concept of working class as used in the GDR has a broad scope, is very differentiated and emphasises the 'process nature' of changes in social structure. According to this concept the working class includes 'the major part of the capitalist wage earners, who have to sell their labour — hence inclusive of most of the employees (but exclusive of the small group of top managers and leading employees with strategic decision-making authority) and workers outside material production. The major part of the intelligentsia still has to be considered a separate stratum — notwithstanding the interrelationship and partial overlap between class and stratum.'[68]

These ideological definitions of concepts should not be dismissed as futile exercises in scholasticism; they are rather an 'instrument for the development of revolutionary class consciousness of the workers under imperialism'. This is seen as important because 'objective membership of the working class' neither leads to solidarity of interests of all the members of a class, nor does it give rise spontaneously to a 'unified class consciousness'.[69] It was increasingly an obligation for the Party to achieve this.

The new Party programme of the SED of 1976 states that the march of the Western capitalist countries towards socialism is irreversible but it inserts an intermediate stage between the two — the establishment of 'anti-monopolist democracy which opens up the road towards socialism'. In this way, it would appear, an attempt is being made to win such adherents in West Germany who are at present not ready to flock to the colours of GDR socialism.

Concepts of this kind are of some importance for policy making. Yet the now more differentiated and more subtle analyses still retain a large ideological component which prevents a more objective view of political, economic and social developments in West Germany and thus reduces the effectiveness of the methods adopted. In essence, if one were to take these ideological concepts at face value, the GDR and its theoreticians of imperialism only needed to wait for the assumed process of concentration in West German 'state monopoly capitalism' to take its pre-ordained course and see how it would ultimately lead to socialism as an exponential form of that capitalism.

8
Foreign Policy and the German Problem

The German problem

As mentioned in the chapter on history the post-war policies of the two German states towards each other went in completely different directions. Whereas West Germany had rejected all suggestions made by the GDR in the early post-war years to achieve reunification in the framework of the People's Congress movement because of the then existing domestic and international political conditions it began to reconsider its attitudes after the building of the Berlin wall on 13 August 1961. As late as in the 1950's attitudes about reunification in the West German government and also broad sections of the population had been influenced by hopes for a solution at the conference table, but the beginning of the 1960s saw the hardening of the conviction that any direct road to reunification was impossible. Hopes that the USSR for one reason or another would abandon the communist-ruled portion of Germany, or that the leadership of the GDR would open the way to reunification due to economic difficulties and because of lack of support among the population, turned out to be illusory. The nuclear stalemate between the superpowers and the building of the Berlin wall demonstrated to the West German public how strongly much of political activity in Europe is directed towards maintenance of the status quo. The Berlin agreement of 17 December 1963 on permits to visit the eastern part of the city, the correspondence between SPD and SED in 1966 concerning an exchange of speakers from the two Parties, as well as the exchange of letters in 1967 between the then West German Chancellor Kiesinger and the former Chairman of the GDR Council of Ministers, Stoph, are all to be interpreted as first steps for an intensification of intra-German contacts within the concept developed by Egon Bahr in 1963 in extension of Kennedy's 'strategy of peace', namely the *Politik der kleinen Schritte* (literally a 'policy of small steps', i.e. gradualism) and *Wandel durch Annäherung* ('change by approximation', i.e. change of the more undesirable aspects of the GDR by dealing with that state directly and creating a firm web of interdependence). In 1968 West Germany extended the offer of making formal declarations on the renunciation of force — as contained in the government's Peace Note of March 1966 — to cover the GDR also.

East Germany reacted to this development by introducing a

separate GDR citizenship in 1967, a socialist penal code in the same year and a new socialist constitution in spring 1968. At the same time intra-German contacts were made more difficult and appeared temporarily obliterated by the East German demand for full international legal recognition.

The *de facto* recognition of the GDR in the government declaration by Chancellor Brandt on 28 October 1969, the meetings between Brandt and Stoph in March 1970 in Erfurt (East Germany) and in May 1970 in Kassel (West Germany) and the conclusion of the Moscow Treaty on 12 August 1970, where the Federal Government took on the obligation unconditionally to respect the territorial integrity of all the states in Europe within their present borders, are some of the most important pointers on the road to the conclusion on 21 December 1972 of the Basic Treaty. This Treaty, which regulates relations between the two German states, represents an important landmark in post-war German history.

The Treaty notwithstanding, the two German states continue to adhere to different views as to what constitutes a nation. As for West Germany the common German experience — or continuity of history — and consciousness of political community form the two essential elements of a nation. In contrast the GDR sees a nation primarily as a 'form of development of the productive forces and culture'. From this concept of nation naturally follows an image of Germany as outlined by Walter Ulbricht on 17 December 1970 in an important address under the title of '25 Years after the Unification of the Working Class', presented to the Commission charged with the preparation of the twenty-fifth anniversary of the SED. This image, which remains valid today, holds that 'The bourgeois German nation, which developed in the process of transition from feudalism to capitalism and which existed in the form of a unified state from 1871 to 1945, does no longer exist. The GDR is the socialist German national state, in which the process of formation of a socialist nation moves towards its perfection. The foreign policy of the GDR aims at creating external conditions favourable for the construction of socialism and to keep the advance towards socialism free from external interference... Whereas the adversary wants to use relations with the GDR so as to approximate the GDR to the FRG under the sign of a fictitious "national commonalty" and to gain a foothold in the GDR for his social democratic theory of society, it is the aim of our policy to establish such relations with the FRG as are unconditionally in accordance with international law, serve the objective and inevitable further delimitation between the two [German] states and hence frustrate all plans for any kinds of "intra-German relations." '

As shown by this quotation the West German policy of *Wandel durch Annäherung* since 1970 has been met by East German attempts at winning acceptance for the theory of two German nations in addition to the thesis of the existence of two German states. SED spokesmen argue in this connection that a separate socialist German nation is being formed in the GDR and that this nation has nothing in common with the dying and decaying bourgeois nation in West Germany. Recently another distinction has been emphasised in the GDR — the difference between nation and nationality. A 'nation' is defined by its class nature and economic system; 'nationality', which for citizens in East and West Germany is 'German', is nevertheless seen as a component of two separate nations.[70]

The West German attitude on the national question was clarified in a decision of the Federal Constitutional Court of 31 July 1973. The decision, which ruled that the Basic Treaty did not violate the Constitution of the Federal Republic, stated that 'If reference is being made today to the "German nation" as a link for the whole of Germany there can be no objection if it is understood to be a synonym for *deutsches Staatsvolk* [the German people making up the state], i.e. if the legal provision [in the Constitution concerning the obligation of Federal German government to strive for reunification] is being observed, and only a different formula has been selected for reasons of political expediency. However, if the new formula of the "German nation" contained *only* the concept of linguistic and cultural unity in the consciousness of the population this would mean abandonment of an inalienable legal position. The latter would be in contradiction to reunification as a goal which the Federal Government is obligated to strive for by all permissible means. The same would be true if reference to four-Power responsibility for Germany as a whole were to mean that in future it [such responsibility] *alone* remained as the legal link for the continued existence of Germany as a whole; the only [legitimate] constitutional interpretation is — as recognised by the Federal Government itself — [the view] that it is a further legal basis for the efforts of the Federal Government to achieve reunification, i.e. an "international legal" *in addition to* a "domestic legal" basis.' (Italics in original.) In conclusion it would be fair to say that the great majority of the population of the GDR shares the view of the Federal Republic on the national question and is motivated by a strong desire for reunification.

The new intra-German policy of the GDR, which goes under the name of 'delimitation' (*Abgrenzung*), from the official East German point of view is nothing but part of foreign policy in general. Delimitation in East German interpretation rests on the 'fact of the existence of two German states with different social structure': in the GDR a socialist German nation is being forged from a basis of changed socio-economic conditions. Delimitation, therefore, is understood to be an objective process. The concept of delimitation has been used quite pointedly and sharply in the GDR presumably so as to destroy any illusions to the effect that détente in Europe could lead to reunification. Delimitation is being regarded as a precondition for the normalization of relations between the two states, which is seen not as a one-time event but a gradual process. Nevertheless, illusions also had to be put into perspective as regards the possibility of joint action by the two German states in matters of high policy: whereas the alliance with the West has priority for West Germany, it is the alliance with the USSR which is predominant in East Germany's priorities. From the point of view of the GDR even the relations with Poland and Czechoslovakia are of greater importance than those with West Germany.

Delimitation of the GDR from West Germany is not to be confused with complete isolation; paradoxically, it is even seen as the very *basis* of cooperation between the two German states. This is true particularly in a sphere where cooperation is seen as not being in conflict with delimitation, namely economics. (Compare the chapter on the economy.)

In its attempts to discover its true identity the GDR is faced with the problem of not being able to take recourse to the ordinary elements of a national state such as language, culture and history: those are elements which it has in common with 'imperialist' West Germany. For this reason it is constantly in search of criteria of differentiation derived from the political and economic system and from ideology.

Another problem for the GDR in its relations with West Germany is the dilemma inherent in the obligation of having to implement the supplementary agreements to the Basic Treaty, which provide for a broad scope of cooperation, and the perceived need of limiting as far as possible the many contacts with West Germany and its citizens. On the one hand the Basic Treaty has removed the last obstacle to international recognition of the GDR but on the other hand it has given rise to a whole new range of expectations among the East German population which the government is unable to meet. It is therefore forced to attempt squaring the circle — to engage in cooperation and increase contacts between the two parts of Germany but to keep in check 'undesirable' repercussions as much as possible. In order to correspond to this aim the GDR adopted a number of measures in the domestic sphere which at least in part are contradictory to the spirit of the treaties between East and West Germany.

Priorities of foreign policy

In its foreign policy the GDR is pursuing one major goal above all — the creation of favourable international conditions for the construction and improvement of socialism. This is a goal that is derived from domestic political needs and it is something the GDR would like to see adopted by the other socialist countries. In fact, GDR foreign policy is firmly tied to that of the latter countries and rests on the following three foundations: 1. the common Marxist-Leninist ideology; 2. membership in the Warsaw Pact; and 3. membership in Comecon.

The GDR bases its foreign policy on doctrines which are valid also for the other socialist countries. These include the following:

1. The relations between the socialist countries are conducted according to the principles of 'socialist internationalism'. These principles are defined as a special form of 'proletarian internationalism' limited to the East European countries, said to be 'qualitatively higher' than ordinary relations in international politics, seen as extending not only to the state level but also to the Party level, and are thus described as being comparable to relations between members of a family. One of the most important elements of socialist internationalism is the concept of sovereignty used. The countries subject to the principle of socialist internationalism do *not* possess individual sovereignty as it is known in the West. Their sovereignty is of a collective kind determined by its class character, i.e. it is shaped by the common claim that it is the working class that is exerting power in the East European countries. In the circumstance of 'counterrevolutionary' developments threatening the rule of the working class in a socialist country, no matter whether in the form of external military interference or domestic disturbance, all the socialist countries are obligated to come to the aid of the country so threatened. This is what happened in Czechoslovakia in 1968. Brezhnev formulated this doctrine on 12 November 1968 at the V Congress of the Polish United Workers' Party as follows: 'Whenever the internal or external forces inimical to socialism attempt to turn the development of any socialist country towards restoration of the capitalist system, whenever there arises a danger to the security of socialism in that country, a danger to the security of the whole socialist community, then this becomes a problem not only for the people of that country but also a common problem — an object of concern for all the socialist countries. It is easily understood that military assistance to a fraternal country for the purpose of removing a danger posed to its socialist system constitutes an extraordinary measure forced upon us. It can only be set in motion by direct actions of the enemies of socialism in the interior of the country and outside its borders —

by acts which constitute a danger for the common interests of the socialist camp.' Moreover, according to Soviet spokesmen the defence of the 'socialist world system' is being regarded as a 'common internationalist duty'. The socialist countries are not to be diverted from carrying out this duty, neither by an 'abstract concept of sovereignty', nor by 'formal observance of the principle of freedom of self-determination'.

2. GDR relations with countries of different social structure (i.e. the capitalist countries) are governed by the principle of 'peaceful coexistence'. This principle is defined as a form of class struggle on a global scale, the role of the bourgeoisie being played by the rich capitalist countries of the West and the role of the proletariat being assumed by the socialist countries (at least in theory; in practice it is the poor developing countries who could be said to constitute the world proletariat). The policy of peaceful coexistence includes competition of the two systems in politics, diplomacy, economics, armaments and culture but it excludes resort to war. The latter is ruled out because it would push the whole world into an abyss. The Cold War, too, is excluded as a principle for the ordering of relations between the socialist and capitalist countries as it is the continuation of war by political means and — as shown by post-war history — has produced neither victors nor vanquished.

Peaceful coexistence is distinguished from Cold War by the ingredient of cooperation for mutual benefit. The principle asserts that broad economic and technological cooperation with the Western industrialized countries does not contradict the world-wide spreading of communism. Thus, as peaceful coexistence contains the *a priori* assumption of world-wide victory of socialism it remains only a matter of deciding on the correct tactical steps on the road to that victory. This means, above all, to create advantageous conditions by shifting the correlation of forces even further in favour of socialism, no matter whether in the economic or military spheres, as regards relative political stability or political consciousness.

Although the struggle between the two systems is being waged in all spheres with the exception of military conflict, the most important aspect in this connection is held to be economic competition. Victory in the economic sphere would mean unambiguous proof that the socialist economic system is more efficient, just and human than the capitalist system. To some extent, therefore, the 'threat' to capitalism can be found in its own deficiencies and insoluble problems.

As long as two opposed socio-economic systems continue to exist, peaceful coexistence is seen by Soviet ideologists as a form of truce. Only victory of communism on a world scale will bring peace in the sense of the word as it is understood in the West. But victory in Soviet and East German perspectives will not be achieved rapidly. The world is said to live in the historical period of transition between capitalism and socialism, and it is thought to be quite possible that this transition will last a hundred years or even longer just as did the earlier transition from feudalism to capitalism. Socialism will triumph in individual countries when the socio-economic conditions are ripe. The majority of people in a particular country will support socialism when it perceives that system as more attractive than capitalism. It is also being acknowledged that this will occur only when the USSR and the GDR have ameliorated all those deficiencies which make their system unattractive to the West.

In the Soviet and East German view there can be no peaceful coexistence in the sphere of ideology. In fact, ideological struggle between the two systems has to be waged with particular vigour in times of peaceful coexistence. This is not seen as a contradiction because via closer contact with each other the two systems come to know each other better than before and they will tend to emphasise more strongly the distinguishing features separating each other.

3. The relations of the GDR with the countries of the Third World are governed by the principle of support for national-liberation movements whose task it is to free the indigenous peoples from oppression by their former colonial masters or from new economic dependencies. This is codified in the new Party prog-ramme of the SED, according to which the 'national and social liberation struggle of the peoples of Asia, Africa and Latin America' constitutes an 'important element of the world revolu-tionary process'. The socialist countries, the international workers' movement in the capitalist countries and the national liberation movements among the coloured peoples form a united front of anti-imperialist struggle. The Party programme also introduced the concept of 'anti-capitalist' path of development as an intermediate stage on the road from national liberation to the construction of a socialist society; this concept is to apply to the peoples of the Third and Fourth Worlds. It is to underline also the East German preference for the ex-colonial peoples to avoid altogether the capitalist stage of development because it carries with it the risk that they will stay too long in that stage.

In further elaboration of these three points, it would be correct to say that the political position of the GDR in the 'socialist community' (i.e. the Warsaw Pact and Comecon) has become stronger than before after the conclusion of the Basic Treaty, international recognition and membership in the United Nations. The replacement of Ulbricht by Honecker in mid-1971 meant an even stronger orientation of the GDR towards the USSR. On the other hand it would be wrong to underestimate the GDR's degree of political influence in the socialist alliance due to its status as the economically most successful country in East Europe; indications of this do surface at times in the form of conflicts of interest between the GDR and USSR.

Some of the expressions of increased integration among the East European countries are the various bilateral cooperation agreements concluded during the last few years in the economic and ideological spheres. (In part, they can be regarded as having been prompted by the West German *Ostpolitik* and the policy of détente, including the European Security Conference and the Vienna conference for the reduction of armed forces and armaments in Central Europe.) In this connection increased cooperation between the GDR and Poland is particularly noteworthy, and so are the links between the GDR and the USSR. The latter has even been codified in the Constitution of the GDR (Article 6, section 2), which states that 'The German Democratic Republic is forever and irrevocably allied with the Union of Soviet Socialist Republics'.

It is difficult to assess the military value of the GDR for the Warsaw Pact. From a strategic point of view the GDR has considerable importance as it rounds off the geographical extent of the alliance: without the GDR the Warsaw Pact would have a very long borderline with NATO all along the Polish and Czechoslovak frontiers. The contribution of the GDR's National People's Army (NVA), too, should not be underrated: it includes 189,000 officers and men of the regular armed forces, as well as 16,000 reserve forces organised in 'police' formations with military functions, 8,500 transport police, 4,500 troops of the Ministry for State Security and 400,000 men in the factory militia. Although the NVA is much smaller than the *Bundeswehr*, the West German equivalent, it is regarded as being highly trained and politically more reliable than in the past. Since 1967-8 the NVA has been integrated into the First Strategic Echelon of the armed forces of the Warsaw Pact. This is of some importance as only politically reliable units are accepted into this echelon.

According to official East German figures, the GDR in 1976 spent US $158 per capita of the population for defence (as compared to US $242 in West Germany); this is the equivalent of 7.8 per cent of total budgetary expenditures (23.5 per cent in West Germany respectively) and constitutes 5.5 per cent of the GDR national income produced (West Germany: 3.7 per cent).[71] As in the Soviet case, however, the official figures do not tell very much about actual defence expenditures, which are likely to be much higher than those officially provided.

In its policy towards the Western countries — after world-wide international legal recognition, with the exception of Israel — the GDR has attempted to free itself from the traditional preoccupation with West Germany and to conduct a policy that is more European in outlook. Indications of this are the participation of the GDR in the European Security Conference and the talks on 'Mutual and Balanced Force Reductions' (MBFR). In the context of these forums the GDR continues its quest for higher political status. The policy of the East European countries in these forums is well coordinated so that differences in national points of view can only be discerned in fine nuances of emphasis. During the foreign ministers' stage of negotiations on the CSCE in July 1973 the GDR, together with Hungary, had the function of presenting a draft declaration of the Conference concerning co-operation in the spheres of economics, trade, science and technology, as well as the protection of the environment. The GDR is very much interested in the MBFR talks in Vienna as its territory accounts for the largest portion of the total area of the Warsaw Pact subject to reductions, not least because of the fact that about 400,000 Soviet troops are stationed in East Germany. Due to the still shaky legitimacy of the regime, reductions agreed upon at the talks would touch the security interests of the GDR more than those of any other East European state affected.

Next to the Scandinavian countries it is France, above all, which belongs to a group of states which were subject to prolonged and strenuous East German efforts for recognition. Parallel to the Soviet appraisal of De Gaulle's foreign policy since 1958 the GDR wanted to encourage as far as possible the General's concept of 'Europe from the Atlantic to the Urals' and the related tendencies of weakening the ties between Western Europe and the United States, the weakening of NATO by withdrawing France from military integration, his veto against further integration and expansion of the Common Market and, finally, his recognition of the Oder-Neisse line as the borders between Poland and the GDR.

The GDR's policy *vis-à-vis* the Third World has been characterized by competition with West Germany's development aid. By making generous offers of aid to selected countries East Germany for years attempted to induce these countries to take the lead on the recognition issue. In this connection, primary emphasis was given to India and the Arab countries. Since the GDR, as noted, has little difficulty to identify with the slogans of national liberation in the Third World it has evoked in some countries a more positive response than West Germany.

In mid-September 1973 both East and West Germany became members of the United Nations — the 133rd and 134th member states respectively. In the eyes of the GDR, UN-membership is the crowning act and reward for years of stubborn efforts in foreign policy for that very purpose. Membership in the UN was regarded as important for two main reasons: first, it was meant to erode the

West German claim of sole recognition; secondly, the GDR
intended, and still intends, to utilize membership in a multilateral
forum as an instrument for enhancing further its new international
respectability.

The GDR — a model state?

When in 1974 the GDR celebrated the twenty-fifth anniversary of
its foundation it asserted that its citizens had constructed a socialist
state in which they could lead a 'dignified human life' — a life
'without exploitation and crises, safe and protected'. In view of the
excesses of the achievement-oriented society in West Germany, its
high technological level, an unemployment rate of 4.8 per cent and
scarcity of ideas of the kind that would inspire enthusiasm and
self-sacrifice among young people (who nevertheless accept democracy, freedom and the rule of law as the natural order of things as
they have grown up enjoying these benefits) the question arises
whether the GDR could serve as a model of development and
improvement for West Germany.

There is doubt whether the East German experience has much
to offer to West Germany in the economic sphere. It appears that
much of the success of the GDR in that sphere has been achieved
not so much *because of* the system of central planning under
socialism but *in spite of it*. Although East German economic
achievements are considerable in comparison with those of the East
European countries, they fade in comparison with West Germany's
economic success and do not prove the case that the command
economy is a useful model for modern industrial society.

As market-type economies (as demonstrated by the West German
example) are more efficient and successful in modern industrial
society than the system of central planning there may be other
possibilities for the GDR's economic system to serve as a model.
For instance, frequent reference is being made in the GDR to 'just'
distribution of the means of production to the extent that private
ownership has been replaced by 'people's' or state ownership.
While this may fulfil formal criteria of 'justice', in practice central
planning can be achieved only at the expense of freedoms, and
indeed a type of state capitalism has developed in the GDR which
makes the 'state monopoly-capitalist' tendencies, as perceived by
East Germany in West Germany, appear as rather harmless. Also,
the identity of people and state, as postulated by GDR ideology, in
reality does not exist. On the contrary: once the state assumes
responsibility for ever more activities on behalf of 'the people' the
citizen will realise some day that he has been reduced to a status of
almost total dependence. In such conditions there is no consolation
in the slogan that the state represents the people. The official

argument in the GDR is that the state's democratic legitimacy has amply been demonstrated by regular elections to popular assemblies. However, such elections do not mitigate the citizen's realization of his own impotence as he is not given choices among political alternatives in genuine democratic elections. Again, there is no consolation in the promise that the political system in the GDR is meant to aid the citizen in achieving genuine freedom and humanity. No matter what the promise, the almost total present-day dependence is felt as being real.

For all these reasons the East German experience does not recommend itself to West Germany. At best it serves to stabilize the latter's social system by inducing it to adopt reforms for the purpose of removing aspects of bias, excess and social injustice and to adapt to changing political and social requirements. It is also possible at times that solutions to problems developed with some success in East Germany can, after due modification, be integrated in the West German system provided the basic principles of a Western parliamentary democracy and a socially-oriented market economy remain untouched. For instance, this could apply to the spheres of health, education and welfare.

The GDR is ruled by leaders who are convinced that they know the laws of development of history as discerned 'scientifically' by Marx and Engels; part of this knowledge is the assumption that mankind will be redeemed because it is progressively developing towards communism. They claim that they are in the process of creating a state on German soil that is constructing socialism on the basis of the recognized laws of development. According to this claim, the GDR belongs to the 'victorious' in history, and West Germany represents a system that in principle is already outmoded and will be superseded by socialism. In practice, however, the threat to 'capitalism' in West Germany by the ideas of Marxism-Leninism is marginal due to the weaknesses of socialism in action.

In essence, the West German rejection of the GDR as a model for economy and society rests on the recognition of the inherent contradictions of the socialist system (although the fact of such contradictions would be strictly denied by East German Communists — as would be the possibility of conflict between individual and collective interests in socialist society). But to what extent can it be argued that the Communist leadership has been successful in instilling a new consciousness in its citizenry? How much dedication is there to Communist ideals? Certainly, there are some seeds which are firmly implanted among youth in the GDR. These include rejection of private ownership in heavy industry and in banking. However, those who were born and raised in the GDR would like to see socialism in their country penetrated by democratic elements. As the Czechoslovak reformers in 1968, and as proclaimed by the

Eurocommunists, young people in the GDR, too, do not accept that socialism and democracy are incompatible.

Almost three decades of socialist reality in the GDR do not leave the citizens with any choice other than adapting to external pressures of various kinds lest they come in direct conflict with administrative measures of the 'first workers' and peasants' state on German soil'. In practice, this means that the majority of common people in the GDR — notwithstanding the intensive and uninterrupted Marxist-Leninist indoctrination — must be regarded as largely apolitical and primarily interested in achieving a high standard of living. In fact, it is fair to say that the main distinguishing feature of the socialist and Western ways of life consists in socialist attitudes compensating for the lower standard of living in the socialist countries. Various forms of political opportunism have developed in GDR society, some of these extending to the state level. Also, the attraction of West Germany among the population in the GDR is such that it reflects negatively on the degree of loyalty of the citizenry — at least in the eyes of the East German leadership. But although the GDR authorities have received an increasing number of visa applications for emigration to West Germany, thus confirming the leadership's doubts about loyalties, the very fact that such applications are being made openly does show some degree of political trust in the government.

For as long as the border between the two German states remains a border between two military alliances, two economic organisations and even two opposed world systems, it is difficult to imagine how reunification could ever be achieved; and although one of the two systems claims that it will supersede the other in a transitional period, possibly lasting several generations, it is even doubtful whether reunification is still a desirable goal in the East. The theory of the existence of two German states (as codified in the Basic Treaty) would lead to the development of two German nations if the new opportunities for increased communication, which have been created recently, were neglected. Thus, in 1977, the GDR registered a total of 7.7 million visits by West Germans and West Berliners — an astoundingly high number that amply documents the continued interest of Germans on both sides of the border in maintaining contact. Such reciprocal interest is a prerequisite for the will to belong to one common nation; without this, it is conceivable that, in different global political conditions, the two German states could find the way open to reunification but would no longer be interested in it.

Abbreviations

BGL	Betriebsgewerkschaftsleitung	Enterprise trade union leadership
BKV	Betriebskollektivvertrag	Enterprise collective agreement
CC		Central Committee
CDU	Christlich-Demokratische Union (Ost)	Christian-Democratic Union (East)
CPSU		Communist Party of the Soviet Union
DBB	Demokratische Bauernpartei Deutschlands	Democratic Peasant Party of Germany
DFD	Demokratischer Frauenbund Deutschlands	Democratic Women's Union of Germany
EOS	Erweiterte Oberschule	Extended Secondary School
FDGB	Freier Deutscher Gewerkschaftsbund	Free German Union of Trade Unions
FDJ	Freie Deutsche Jugend	Free German Youth
GPD	Gärtnerische Produktionsgenossenschaft	Market-gardening producers' cooperative
GST	Gesellschaft für Sport und Technik	Society for Sport and Technical Affairs
HO	Handelsorganisation	Trade organisation
KB	Kulturbund	Cultural Union
LDPD	Liberal-Demokratische Partei Deutschlands	Liberal-Democratic Party of Germany
LPG	Landwirtschaftliche Produktionsgenossenschaft	Agricultural producers' cooperative
NDPD	National-Demokratische Partei Deutschlands	National-Democratic Party of Germany
NES		New Economic System
NSDAP	Nationalsozialistische Deutsche Arbeiterpartei	National Socialist (Nazi) Party
NVA	Nationale Volksarmee	National People's Army
PGH	Produktionsgenossenschaft des Handwerks	Skilled Craft producers' cooperative
POS	Zehnklassige allgemeinbildende polytechnische Oberschule	Ten-year general polytechnical secondary school
SAG	Sowjetische Aktien-Gesellschaft	Soviet joint-stock company
SBZ	Sowjetische Besatzungszone Deutschlands	Soviet Occupation Zone of Germany
SED	Sozialistische Einheitspartei Deutschlands	Socialist Unity Party of Germany

SGB	Sozialistischer Grosshandelsbetrieb	Socialist wholesale enterprise
SMAD	Sowjetische Militär-administration in Deutschland	Soviet Military Administration in Germany
SPD	Sozialdemokratische Partei Deutschlands	Social Democratic Party of Germany
VEB	Volkseigener Betrieb	Nationalised enterprise
VEB	Volkseigenes Gut	Nationalised estate
VVB	Vereinigung Volkseigner Betriebe	Association of nationalised enterprises

Military and Economic Data

ARMED FORCES IN 1975

Federal Republic of Germany		*German Democratic Republic*	
Population		Population	
(excl. W. Berlin)[1]	59,967m.	(incl. E. Berlin)[3]	16,891m.
Land forces	340,000	Land forces	98,000
Air forces	111,000	Air forces	28,000
Sea forces	39,000	Sea forces	17,000
		Border troops	46,000
Total Federal forces[2]	490,000	Total People's Army	189,000
= 0.82% of the population		= 1.13% of the population	
Reservists	c. 2.0m.	Reservists[4]	c. 1.0m
= 3.3% of the population		= 5.9% of the population	
Other armed forces:		Other armed forces:	
Federal border		Emergency police	16,000
guards	20,000	Transport police	8,500
Provinces' emergency		Ministry for State	
police	20,000	Security Troops	4,500
	40,000		29,000
Militia	none	Militia[4]	
		(enterprise fighting	
		groups)	400,000
		= 2.4% of the population	
Pre-military training	none	Pre-military training	400,000
Period of military		Period of military	
service	15 months	service	18 months

NOTES
[1] West Berlin citizens, in accordance with the Four-Power status of Berlin, are not called up to the Federal Forces.
[2] Excluding central military Federal Forces headquarters with around 11,000 staff.
[3] East Berlin residents are called up to the National People's Army of the GDR.
[4] 1972

Source: *Zahlenspiegel* (A comparison of the Federal Republic of Germany and the German Democratic Republic). Published by the Federal Ministry for Intra-German Relations. Bonn – Bad Godesburg, 1976, p. 8.

PRICES AND PURCHASING POWER
OF ONE HOUR'S WAGES (NET) (1976)

Commodity	Unit	Retail prices		Working time necessary to buy[1]	
		FRG (DM)	GDR (Marks)	FRG (hours/minutes)	GDR
Rye bread (standard)	1 kg.	2.20	0.52	0/14	0/07
White flour (type W 405)	1 kg.	1.20	1.32	0/08	0/18
Refined sugar	1 kg.	1.65	1.64	0/11	0/23
Butter	1 kg.	9.00	10.00	0/58	2/18
Margarine (quality)	1 kg.	4.00	4.00	0/26	0/55
Eggs	each	0.26	0.34	0/02	0/05
Milk (3% fat content)[2]	0.5 l.	0.51	0.36	0/03	0/05
Cheese (Gouda)[3]	1 kg.	9.50	10.00	1/02	2/18
Pork (cutlet)	1 kg.	11.00	8.00	1/11	1/50
Sausage	1 kg.	11.40	6.80	1/14	1/34
Potatoes	5 kg.	3.40	0.85	0/22	0/12
Red Cabbage	1 kg.	1.38	0.44	0/09	0/06
Apples (medium quality)	1 kg.	1.26	1.97	0/08	0/27
Lemons	1 kg.	2.28	5.00	0/15	1/09
Chocolate (milk)	100 g	1.04	3.85	0/07	0/53
Coffee (medium quality)	1 kg.	23.60	70.00	2/33	16/06
Brandy (38%)	0.71 l.	11.80	11.30	1/17	3/59
Cigarettes (medium price)	20	2.70	3.20	0/18	0/44
Man's shirt (artificial fibre)	1	19.90	46.80	2/09	10/46
Lady's stockings	1 pair	3.45	4.00	0/22	0/55
Lady's tights	1 pair	3.65	18.00	0/24	4/08
Children's shoes	1 pair	28.20	18.00	3/03	4/08
Washing machine	1	498.00	1450.00	53/50	333/20
Vacuum cleaner (with accessories)	1	165.00	195.00	17/50	44/50
Refrigerator (170 litres)	1	338.00	1400.00	36/32	321/50
TV set (black and white, table model) 61 or 62 cm tube	1	530.00	2050.00	57/18	471/16
Passenger car[4]	1	8570.00	23500.00	926/29	5402/18
Railway weekly ticket, 2nd class, 15km, without surcharge	1	13.00	2.50	1/24	0/34
Electricity (domestic tariff)[5]	75 kwh.	21.40	8.00	2/19	1/50

NOTES

[1] Based on the average net hourly earnings of an industrial worker of DM9.25 in the Federal Republic and 4.35 Mark in the GDR (1975).
[2] Milk in 0.5 litre bottles, 3% fat content in FRG, 2.5% in GDR.
[3] 40% fat content in FRG; 30% in GDR.
[4] FRG and GDR: Polski-Fiat 125.
[5] Including fixed charge in both FRG and GDR.

Source: Federal Ministry for Intra-German Relations.

INDICATORS OF THE ECONOMIC DEVELOPMENT OF THE GDR

| | Growth over previous year, % | | | | | | Total growth, % | | | |
| | | | | 1977 | | 1978 | 1971-75 | | | 1976-80 |
	1974	1975	1976	(plan)	(actual)	(plan)	(actual)	(plan)	(directives)	(law)
National Income produced*	6.4	5.0	3.7	5.5	5.2	5.2	29.9	27	27-30	27.9
Industry:										
commodity production	7.4	6.4	5.9	5.1	5.4	5.7	37	34	34-36	34.0
labour productivity	6.3[7]	5.5[7]	6.0[8]	5.1	5.2	5.0	(29)	35	30-32	30.0
Construction output	9.7	7.5	6.8	6.2	6.4	5.7	27.6	27	32-33	37.2
Gross capital investment	4.2	3.8[5]	6.8[9]	6.5[9]	6.0[9]	2.1	(23)	16	29-31	30.1
Retail trade turnover[4]										
total	6.1	3.5	4.3	4.0	4.3	4.0	28	22[1]	20-22[2]	21.5
foodstuffs	4.2	3.0	3.1	—	3.9	3.5	19	16[3]	—	—
industrial goods	8.2	4.0	5.6	—	4.7	4.4	40	30[3]	—	—
Foreign trade turnover[4]	19.6	16.2[2]	14.0	8.7	7.0	11.0	75.7	—	—	—
Exports	16.3	—	—	—	—	—	72.6	—	—	—
Imports	22.8	—	—	—	—	—	78.9	—	—	—
Net money incomes of the population	4.8	4.0	4.0	4.0	5.4	4.0	27	22	20-22	21.4

NOTES

[1] Commodities for the population
[2] Commodity turnover for supplying the population
[3] Including increases in stocks in consumer goods trade network
[4] Total imports and exports, including intra-German trade, excluding services, in foreign trade Marks at current prices
[5] Excluding general repairs
[6] Real increase = 7%
[7] Gross output per blue and white collar workers (excluding apprentices)
[8] For industrial ministries
[9] Including investment in Comecon countries

*National income produced is the total of material goods and productive services produced by society in a year, less those used in production (depreciation, rent, hire charges, use of materials and productive services).

Source: Federal Ministry for Intra-German Relations

THE POSITION OF THE GDR WITHIN COMECON, 1975
(selected data)

	GDR	Bulgaria	Cuba	Mongolia	Poland	Rumania	Czecho-slovakia	USSR	Hungary
Surface area (km^2)	108,178	110,912	110,922	1,565,000	312,677	237,500	127,877	22,402,200	93,030
Population (1,000)	16,850	8,722	9,332	1,446	34,022	21,247	14,802	254,393	10,540
Population per km^2	156	79	84	1	109	89	116	11	113
National product index (1970 = 100)	130	146	–	138	159	171	131	132	135
National product per capita population (1970 = 100)	132	142	–	120	152	163	127	126	132
Contribution to national product (%)									
industry	59.1	51	–	24.7	52.1	57.1	64.4	52.7	47
agriculture	11.1	22	–	22.4	12.6	16.6	8.3	16.8	16.3
Employed national income consumption (%)	77.7	67.5	–	62.4	62.8	–	70.7	73.6	70.3
Gross industrial production index (1970 = 100)	137	155	150	155	164	184	138	143	136
annual growth rate (%)	6.4	9.6	11.1	7	11.2	12.4	6.7	7.5	4.8
Labour productivity, industry index (1970 = 100)	130	139	–	137	145	136	134	134	135
Industrial production									
electricity (GWh)	84,505	25,235	6,583	818	96,862	53,721	59,277	1,038,607	20,457
petroleum (1000 t.)	–	122	–	–	553	14,590	142	481,766	2,006
crude steel (1000 t.)	6,472	2,265	298	–	15,004	9,549	14,323	141,344	3,671
private vehicles	159,147	15,004	–	–	164,013	68,013	175,411	1,201,260	–
household refrigerators (1,000)	526.7	182	50	–	736.5	331.8	365.6	5,577.3	431.2
household washing machines (1,000)	373.9	73.3	–	–	619.9	178.3	267.1	3,286	164.4

THE POSITION OF THE GDR WITHIN COMECON, 1975 *continued*

Industrial production *continued*									
television sets (1,000)	509	124	26	–	971	512	445	6,960	400
shoes (mill. pairs)	79	23.7	21.2	1.8	134.3	69.4	113.6	698.1	43.1
textiles (mill. m²)	745	442	144	1.3	1,543	848	873	9,804	474
Vegetable foodstuffs production cereals and legumes (1,000 t.)	8,988	7,792	470	483	19,819	15,377	9,423	140,118	12,359
Animal foodstuffs production meat (1000 t. slaughtered weight)	1,718	657	–	225	3,062	1,328	1,349	15,060	1,474
Foreign trade turnover (mill. roubles)	15,930	7,521	5,540	349	17,057	7,960	12,171	50,699	8,645
with COMECON countries	10,550	5,551	3,070	336	8,485	3,022	8,036	26,248	5,714
College and university students per 10,000 population 1975/6	81	127	87	94	137	77	104	190	102
Doctors per 10,000 population	23.6	25.7	12.1	19.9	21.7	15.9	27	32.7	24.9

Sources: Compiled by the author from: *Statistisches Jahrbuch 1977 der Deutschen Demokratischen Republik* (Annual statistical report of the GDR), 22nd. year, published by the Staatliche Zentralverwaltung für Statistik, Berlin (East), 1977.

PRODUCTION OF SELECTED ARTICLES, 1976

Item	Unit	Federal Republic of Germany	GDR	Comparison of production per inhabitant (Federal Republic of Germany = 100)
Electrical energy	TWh	334	89	97
Soft coal	Mill. t.	135	247	670
Petrol	1,000 t.	23,297	2,982	47
Diesel fuel	1,000 t.	9,768	5,108	192
Synthetic materials	1,000 t.	6,497	694	39
Man-made fibres	1,000 t.	771	118	56
Cement	mill. t.	36.3	11.3	114
Crude steel	mill. t.	41.8	6.7	56
Grinding machines	unit	21,940	4,666	78
Rolling stock	unit	10,564	7,150	248
Heavy goods vehicles	1,000	288	36	46
Private vehicles	1,000	3,548	164	17
Household washing machines	1,000	1,768	390	81
Television sets	1,000	3,726	561	55
Cameras	1,000	3,472	844	89
Wood fibre board	1,000 m^3	6,125	622	40
Paper	1,000 t.	5,340	801	56
Crockery	1,000 t.	91.6	39.6	158
Pianos	1,000 t.	27.7	25.1	332
Outdoor shoes	mill. pair	100.6	42.7	155
Cotton fabric	mill. m^2	798	422	194
Sugar	1,000 t.	2,401	666	102
Butter	1,000 t.	506	277	200
Flour	1,000 t.	3,775	1,318	128
Beer	mill. hl.	91.4	21.2	85
Non-alcoholic beverages	mill. hl.	66.2	12.0	66
Cigarettes	1,000 mill.	149	20	49

Source: Federal Ministry for Intra-German Relations

INDEX OF CONSUMER DURABLES PER 100 HOUSEHOLDS

	Federal Republic	*GDR*
	1973	*1974*
Private vehicles[1]	55	24
Motor cycles[2]	7	48
Radio sets[3]	99	96
Television sets[3]	89	80
colour TV sets	15	4[4]
Electric refrigerators	93	80
Electric washing machines	75	71
fully automatic machines	59	1[4]
Deep-freezes	28	3
Sewing machines, all types	66	54
Vacuum cleaners, all types	91	87
Telephones[5]	51	17

NOTES
[1] Including estate cars, not including company and official cars
[2] Including motor scooters and mopeds
[3] Reception licences issued
[4] Results of a poll held in 1975
[5] Private main lines

Source: Federal Ministry for Intra-German Relations

References

1   *Ökonomische Geographie der Deutschen Demokratischen Republik. Bevölkerung, Siedlungen, Wirtschaftsbereiche* (Gotha, 1970), p. 15.

2   Staatliche Zentralverwaltung für Statistik (ed.), *Statistisches Jahrbuch der Deutschen Demokratischen Republik, 1977* (Berlin [East], 1977), p. 1.

3   Bundesministerium für innerdeutsche Beziehungen (ed.), *Bericht der Bundesregierung und Materialien zur Lage der Nation, 1971* (Bonn, 1971), pp. 77f.

4   Deutsches Institut für Wirtschaftsforschung (ed.), *DDR-Wirtschaft: Eine Bestandsaufnahme* (Frankfurt/M, 1974), pp. 143f.

5   Hans Bichler and Clemens Szamatolski, *Landwirtschaft in der DDR: Agrar-politik und Landwirtschaft in einem sozialistischen Industriestaat* (Berlin, 1973), pp. 75-82.

6   *Tribüne* (Berlin [East], 9 February 1976).

7   'Schaffendes Volk in Stadt und Land! Männer und Frauen! Deutsche Jugend!' (Appeal by the CC of the KPD of 11 June 1945), in C. Berthold and E. Diehl (ed.), *Revolutionäre deutsche Partei-programme: Vom Kommunistischen Manifest zum Programm des Sozialismus* (Berlin [East] 1963), pp. 191-200.

8   Theo Stammen (ed.), *Einigkeit und Recht und Freiheit: Westdeutsche Innen-politik 1945 bis 1955* (Munich, 1965), pp. 111f.

9   'Der Weg zum Wiederaufbau Deutschlands', speech by the Chairman of the KPD, Wilhelm Pieck, at a mass meeting in Berlin on 19 July 1945, in *Einheitsfront der antifaschistisch-demokratischen Parteien* (Berlin [East], 1945), p. 54.

10   Anton Ackermann, 'Gibt es einen besonderen deutschen Weg zum Sozialismus?', in *Einheit* (Berlin [East], No. 1 (1945), esp. pp. 22f and 30f.

11   Official Record of the Negotiations of the First Party Conference of the Socialist Unity Party of Germany, 25-28 January 1949, in the Werner-Seelenbinger-Halle in Berlin (Berlin [East], 1949).

12   *Kleines politisches Wörterbuch* (Berlin [East], 1967), p. 430.

13   Institut für Marxismus-Leninismus beim ZK der SED (ed.), *Geschichte der deutschen Arbeiterbewegung in acht Bänden*, Vol. VI (Berlin [East], 1968), pp. 358f.

14   Akademie für Staats- und Rechtswissenschaft der DDR und das Institut für Staats- und Rechtstheorie an der Akademie der Wissenschaften der DDR (ed.), *Wörterbuch zum sozialistischen Staat* (Berlin [East], 1974), p. 287.

15   As quoted by Ernst Deuerlein (ed.), *DDR: Geschichte und Bestandsaufnahme*, 3rd edn. (Munich, 1971), p. 120.

16   Ibid., p. 89.

17   Stefan Doernberg, *Kurze Geschichte der DDR*, 3rd edn. (Berlin [East], 1968), p. 448.

18 Deuerlein, op. cit., p. 221.

19 Kurt Hager, 'Die entwickelte sozialistische Gesellschaft', in *Einheit*, No. 11, (Berlin [East], 1971), p. 1215.

20 Erich Honecker, *Bericht des Zentralkomitees der SED an den IX Parteitag der Sozialistischen Einheitspartei Deutschlands* (Dresden, 1976), pp. 161f.; 'Unsere Partei in Fakten und Zahlen', in *Einheit*, No. 10 (1973), p. 1189; Staatliche Zentralverwaltung für Statistik (ed.), *Statistisches Jahrbuch der Deutschen Demokratischen Republik, 1976*, (Berlin [East], 1976), pp. 443-6; *Neues Deutschland*, 4 June 1976.

21 Peter Christian Ludz, 'Der IX Parteitag der SED: Ein Rückblick', in *Deutschland Archiv* (Cologne), Special Issue (1976), pp. 14f.

22 *Kleines politisches Wörterbuch* (Berlin [East], 1973), p. 927.

23 *Neues Deutschland*, 20 December 1976.

24 Law on Elections for the People's Representatives of the German Democratic Republic of 24 June 1976, paras. 15-21.

25 Decree of the *Staatsrat* of the German Democratic Republic on Elections to the *Volkskammer* and Local People's Representatives of the German Democratic Republic (Electoral Decree) of 31 July 1963, as revised on 2 July 1965, para. 27.

26 Constitution of the GDR, art. LVII, section 2.

27 See note 23 and *Neues Deutschland*, 21 September 1976.

28 *Die Volkskammer der Deutschen Demokratischen Republik* (Berlin [East], 1977), pp. 58-61.

29 *Berliner Zeitung* (Berlin [East]), 22 September 1976.

30 See Gero Neugebauer, 'Die Volkskammer der DDR', in *Zeitschrift für Parlamentsfragen* (Düsseldorf), No. 3 (1974), pp. 386-411, and Eberhard Schneider, 'Die Volksvertretungen in der DDR', in *Zeitschrift für Politik* (Cologne), No. 2 (1975), pp. 183-201.

31 See note 29.

32 *Neues Deutschland*, 10 March 1972.

33 'Thesen zum Wesen und zur Entwicklung des sozialistischen Rechts', presented at the University of Halle, in *Staat und Recht* (Berlin [East], 1963), pp. 1842f; see also 'Gesetz über die Verfassung' of 1 November 1974.

34 Georg Brunner, *Einführung in das Recht der DDR* (Munich, 1975), pp. 98-101.

35 Bericht der Bundesregierung. . .1972, op. cit., p. 291.

36 *Die Konfliktkommission: Erläuterung der Konfliktkommissions-ordnung und eine Auswahl von gesetzlichen Bestimmungen, Richtlinien und Beschlüssen zur Tätigkeit der Konfliktkommissionen*, 3rd edn. (Berlin [East], 1971).

37 Heinz Rausch and Theo Stammen, *DDR: Das politische, wirtschaftliche und soziale System* (Munich, 1973), p. 234; Bundesministerium für inner-deutsche Beziehungen (ed.), *DDR-Handbuch* (Cologne, 1975), p. 483.

38 *Kleines politisches Wörterbuch*, op. cit., pp. 248, 490, 670 and 919. Zahlenspiegel. Ein Vergleich. Bundesministerium für innerdeutsche Beziehungen (ed.), *Bundesrepublik Deutschland — Deutsche Demokratische Republik*, 5th edn. (Bonn, 1976), p. 16.

40 Gert Leptin, 'Korrelation der Kräfte — ein Ost-West-Vergleich der Wirtschaftspotentiale', in *Rissener Rundbrief* (Hamburg), (February 1977).

41 *Neues Deutschland*, 17 December 1976 and 22/23 January 1977; *Frankfurter Allgemeine Zeitung*, 24 January 1977.

42 As calculated by the author on the basis of *Statistisches Jahrbuch der Deutschen Demokratischen Republik, 1976*, op. cit., pp. 265f.

43 Radio GDR II on 17 February 1975.

44 See *Neuer Weg* (Berlin [East]), No. 3 (1975).

45 Peter Christian Ludz, *Deutschlands doppelte Zukunft: Bundesrepublik und DDR in der Welt von morgen. Ein politischer Essay* (Munich, 1974), p. 721.

46 Bulletin des Presse- und Informationsamtes der Bundesregierung, 1978.

47 Helmut Klein, *Bildung in der DDR. Grundlagen, Entwicklungen, Probleme* (Hamburg, 1974), pp. 109-13. The author is Professor of Pedagogy at the Humboldt University in East Berlin.

48 Werner Kienitz (ed.), *Einheitlichkeit und Differenzierung im Bildungswesen* (Berlin [East], 1971), p. 314.

49 Bericht der Bundesregierung...1971, op. cit., p. 213.

50 Gert-Joachim Glaessner, Herwig Haase and Ralf Rytlewski, *Student und Studium in der DDR: Studentische Politik, Informationen, Materialen, Berichte*, Forschungsinstitut der Friedrich-Ebert Stiftung (Bonn-Bad Godesberg, 1971), Nos. 7-8, pp. 7-15 and 34-40.

51 Werner Lamberz, 'Die Massenverbundenheit unserer Partei und die Wirksamkeit von Agitation und Propaganda', in *Einheit* (Berlin [East]), No. 11 (1974), p. 1230.

52 Staatliche Zentralverwaltung für Statistik (ed.), *Statistisches Jahrbuch der Deutschen Demokratischen Republik, 1977*, (Berlin [East], 1977), p. 375. Statistisches Bundesamt (ed.), *Statistisches Jahrbuch 1977 für die Bundesrepublik Deutschland*, (Stuttgart, 1977), S. 365.

53 Akademie für Gesellschaftswissenschaften beim ZK der KPdSU, Institut für Gesellschaftswissenschaften beim ZK der SED (ed.), *Die entwickelte sozialistische Gesellschaft: Wesen und Kriterien — Kritik revisionistischer Konzeptionen* (Berlin [East], 1973).

54 Nikolai W. Faddejew, 'W.I. Lenin und die sozialistische ökonomische Integration', in Werner Sydow (ed.), *Forschung und Entwicklung im RGW: Aktuelle Fragen* (Berlin [East], 1974), p. 14.

55 Institut für Gesellschaftswissenschaften beim ZK der SED (ed.), *Der Imperialismus der BRD* (Berlin [East], 1972), p. 95. See *Widersprüche und Tendenzen im Herrschaftssystem der BRD* (Berlin [East], 1973) and Gretchen Binus, 'Internationale Konzerne und Staat im kapitalistischen Internationalisierungsprozess', in *IPW — Berichte*, No. 8 (1976), pp. 24-33.

56 Gerhard Hahn, 'Imperialistische Ideologen und die friedliche Koexistenz', *Einheit* (Berlin [East]), No. 8 (1972), p. 999.

57 *Politische Ökonomie des heutigen Monopolkapitalismus* (Berlin [East], 1972), p. 847.

58 Dieter Klein, 'Systemauseinandersetzung: Zur Theorie des Klassenkampfes zwischen Sozialismus und Kapitalismus', in *Forum* (Berlin [East]), No. 17 (1972), p. 9.

59 Peter Hess, 'Zum sozialistischen Inhalt der gegenwärtigen Entwicklungsetappe der allgemeinen Krise des Kapitalismus', in *IPW — Berichte* (Berlin [East]), No. 8 (1972), p. 8; see also Authors' Collective, 'Die ökonomische Lage in den imperialistischen Ländern 1975/Anfang 1976', in *IPW — Berichte* No. 9, (1976), pp. 26-41.

60 Hess, op. cit., pp. 9f. See also 'Friedliche Koexistenz — ideologischer Kampf: Überarbeitete Materialien des wissenschaftlichen Kolloquiums vom 14-15. 2. 1973 in Berlin', in *IPW — Forschungshefte*, No. 2 (Berlin [East], 1973), pp. 32 and 39-43.

61 *Ideologie des Sozialdemokratismus der Gegenwart* (Berlin [East], 1971), p. 353.

62 Hans-Joachim Höhner, 'Krisenzyklus unter dem Einfluss staatsmonopolistischer Kapitalentwertung', in *IPW — Berichte*, No. 6 (Berlin [East], 1972), pp. 2-13.

63 Klaus Franke, 'Konjunktur und Krise in der BRD heute', in *IPW — Berichte*, No. 2 (Berlin [East], 1973), pp. 23-31.

64 *Der Imperialismus*. . .op. cit., p. 300.

65 W.I. Lenin, *Werke* (Berlin [East]), Vol. XXXI, p. 86; Vol. XV, p. 444; Vol. X, p. 243.

66 *Der Imperialismus*. . .op. cit., pp. 624, 626 and 627.

67 *Ibid.*, pp. 446 and 626.

68 'Neue Tendenzen staatsmonopolistischer Herrschaftssicherung', in *IPW — Berichte*, No. 3 (Berlin [East], 1972), pp. 41-43; see also 'Klassentheorie und Klassendefinition', *ibid.*, No. 4 (1972), p. 43.

69 Der Imperialismus. . .op. cit., p. 44. See also Jürgen Kuczynski, *Klassen und Klassenkämpfe im imperialistischen Deutschland und in der BRD* (Berlin [East], 1972), p. 103.

70 Alfred Kosing und Walter Schmidt, 'Nation und Nationalität in der DDR', in *Neues Deutschland*, 15-16 February 1975.

71 *The Military Balance 1976/77*, International Institute for Strategic Studies (London, 1976).

Some Books in English on the GDR

Baylis, Thomas., *The Technical Intelligentsia and the East German Élite: Legitimacy and Social Change in Mature Communism*, Berkeley, 1974.

Croan, Melvin, *East Germany: The Soviet Connection*, Beverly Hills, 1976.

Herspring, Dale Roy, *East German Civil-Military Relations: The Impact of Technology, 1949-1972*, New York, 1973.

Ludz, Peter Christian, *The Changing Party Elite in East Germany*, Cambridge, Mass., 1972.

Merkl, Peter H., *German Foreign Policies, West and East: On the Threshold of a New European Era*, Santa Barbara, Calif., 1974.

Schweigler, Gebhard, *National Consciousness in a Divided Germany*, Beverly Hills, 1975.

Starrels, John M. and Mallinckrodt, Anita M., *Politics in the German Democratic Republic*, New York, 1975.

Steele, Jonathan, *Socialism with a German Face*, London, 1977.

Sontheimer, Kurt and Bleek, Wilhelm, *The Government and Politics of East Germany*, New York, 1976.

Wettig, Gerhard, *Community and Conflict in the Socialist Camp: the Soviet Union, East Germany and the German Question 1965-72*, London, 1975.

Index